Your
Altar

About the Author

Sandra Kynes describes herself as an explorer because she likes finding underlying similarities and connections, then crafting new ways to interact with the world around her. Looking at things a little differently has resulted in five books thus far. Her curiosity has taken her on many travels and to live in New York City, Europe, England, and New England. In addition to ancient texts such as *The Mabinogion*, Celtic history, myth, and magic, her inquisitiveness has led her to explore a range of spiritual practices. She is a yoga instructor, massage therapist, and Reiki practitioner.

Your Altar

Creating a Sacred Space for Prayer and Meditation

Sandra Kynes

Llewellyn Publications
Woodbury, Minnesota

First Edition
First Printing, 2007

Author photo by Lyle Koehnlein, Fidelio Photography
Book design by Joanna Willis
Cover design and photography by Kevin R. Brown
Interior illustrations by Llewellyn art department

Llewellyn is a registered trademark of Llewellyn Worldwide, Ltd.

Library of Congress Cataloging-in-Publication Data
Kynes, Sandra, 1950–
    Your altar: creating a sacred space for prayer and meditation / Sandra Kynes.—1st ed.
        p.   cm.
    Includes bibliographical references and index.
    ISBN-13: 978-0-7387-1105-8
    1. Spiritual life. 2. Sacred space. 3. Altars. I. Title.
    BL624.K965 2007
    203´.7—dc22
                                                                                        2007030537

Llewellyn Publications
A Division of Llewellyn Worldwide, Ltd.
2143 Wooddale Drive, Dept. 978-0-7387-1105-8
Woodbury, MN 55125-2989, U.S.A.
www.llewellyn.com

Printed in the United States of America

This book is dedicated to the memory of Reverend R. Paul Mueller

Also by Sandra Kynes

Gemstone Feng Shui
A Year of Ritual
Whispers from the Woods

Forthcoming

Sea Magic
(June 2008)

Contents

Illustrations

Figures

Tables

Illustrations

Introduction

The concept of an altar dates to a time in prehistory when people began making offerings to their deities and needed a special place in which to do it. While we might think that this occurred in biblical times in one of the classical civilizations of the Mediterranean, the use of altars can be traced back possibly tens of thousands of years to a cave in France.

Many early altars have been found in conjunction with tombs and other places of burial. While this may seem untoward to the modern mind, entering a tomb for ritual or worship was symbolic of surrendering oneself and re-entering the womb of Mother Earth. Re-emerging afterward represented rebirth and renewal. Ceremony or prayer within a burial sanctuary provided continuity in the cycle of life, death, and rebirth. Altars then and now have served as places where offerings and sacrifices are made—physically and symbolically.

Through the ages, the use of altars has been both communal and private. Although home altars seem more prevalent in certain faiths, in recent years their use has become more widespread, regardless of one's spiritual path.

While altars and their purpose have evolved over the millennia, their use seems to fulfill a fundamental need that transcends spiritual orientation.

There is a certain power to an altar. It is not just a thing that holds a collection of objects. Intention and energy transforms an altar into a space that transcends the mundane world. When we use it, we step outside the boundaries of our everyday lives. When we sit in front of an altar, we place ourselves in the presence of the Divine, as well as spirits and ancestors, and we open ourselves to seek and search for answers to questions that guide our souls.

As a central part of ritual and worship, an altar is a place of spiritual encounter. It serves as a reminder of our contact with the Divine as well as contact with our inner souls. In meditation, we seek to explore our interior life—to go beyond the mind to find our essential self. The simple question of "Who am I?" is not easy to answer.

Using an altar strikes a familiar chord within us. We may not understand why this happens, but we can sense a shift of energy away from ordinary awareness. Altars hold objects of inspiration and devotion, personal and sacred, resulting in a space that visibly and energetically links the spiritual and physical worlds and provides clues to our innermost thoughts and feelings. The Greek word *gnosis* is usually translated as "knowledge"; however, it can also be translated as "insight." According to Elaine Pagels, "Gnosis involves an intuitive process of knowing oneself."[1] An altar becomes a tool for gnosis—knowledge that comes from spiritual insight and self-illumination.

In the past, the sacred and secular were not so rigidly segregated. This is not the case in our present-day world, but having a place where these aspects of our lives come together can be a means for finding balance. This meeting point of spiritual and mundane energies can provide an orientation or anchor in the world—a place to hold on to and come back to for personal strength and exploration. The things that we place on an altar become symbolic of what is going on in our hearts and minds. Because of

---

1 Elaine Pagels, *The Gnostic Gospels*, xix.

the energies that converge there, an altar is not a passive space: there is constant interaction.

In addition to providing a place for worship, an altar also functions as a tool for exploration and growth. Like a labyrinth, an altar top itself can act as a "blueprint for the psyche to meet the soul."[2] An altar is a place where you lay out your intentions—put your cards on the table, so to speak—to manifest particular energies into your life. In describing how Peruvian shamans interact with their altars, Jim DeKorne said that the altar top functioned like a "game board, a symbolic paradigm against which the ritual is played."[3]

This book is about using the altar as a game board, for lack of a better term. The words "game board" are not meant to be frivolous or irreverent, but rather they are a way to convey the concept of a matrix for an altar and a different form of meditation practice. Dividing the altar top into multiple sections and using them to focus a flow of intention allows the altar to function as a powerful and symbolic tool not unlike Buddhist mandalas (sacred circles),[4] classical Christian icons, and Hindu yantras.[5]

A Survey on Home Altars

While working on this book, I conducted a survey (albeit unscientific) concerning the use of home altars. I found people practicing an eclectic mix of spiritual paths. Some were eclectic within the Pagan pantheons, and others practiced blendings of religious traditions. The altars themselves varied from dedicated tables and shelves (and in some instances rooms for meditation, prayer, ritual, and yoga) to shared space on a desk or table that was needed for everyday things. The bedroom was the place most often named

---

2 Dr. Lauren Artress, *Walking a Sacred Path*, 147.

3 Jim DeKorne, *Psychedelic Shamanism*, 139.

4 A mandala is a geometric pattern or diagram used to quiet and focus the mind for meditation. Stephen P. Huyler, *Meeting God*, 264.

5 Huyler describes a yantra as a "symbolic formula of lines used to attract the energy of a deity into a sacred space." Ibid., 204.

as the location for an altar, with the living room a close second. Dens, finished basements, and home offices are also common places.

About 50 percent of the people surveyed kept more than one altar. Some of these had separate purposes—for example, one for prayer and one for meditation, and one general-purpose altar in a "public" room of a house and another for personal use in a bedroom. A few people bridge the sacred and secular gap by keeping a "mini altar" at work.

The items that people keep on their altars range widely and do not appear to be proscribed according to faith. If anything, there is an interfaith mix of symbols and objects. For example, Christians and eclectic Pagans are just as likely to have a statue of Buddha as Buddhists. A person who described their current spiritual practice as nonspecific keeps a statue of Jesus. Many people use objects from nature on their altars, and a high percentage of non-Pagans reported that one use of their altar was as a reminder of the cycle of the seasons. More than 95 percent of those surveyed said that they are the only one to use their altars. Most people's altars are permanent but do change from time to time or with the seasons. In addition, many people take an item or several along when they travel.

The most common reason reported for keeping an altar was to serve as a reminder of one's spiritual path. This was followed by a place of focus for meditation, a place to connect with the Divine, a place of focus for prayer, and a sacred place for ritual or ceremony. A little over 30 percent have dedicated their altars to specific gods, groups of gods (sometimes interfaith groupings), saints, ancestors, animals, birds, teachers, kings, queens, and warriors. My conclusion from the survey is that domestic altars are alive and well and here to stay.

The Altars

The one-part altar layouts take us from the outer reaches of the void of creation to the well of creativity that lies within us. One—complete in itself—can help us work with the three-dimensional energy of the pyramid or the strength of our own seat of will. The one-part altar also aids in directing energy toward or away from us.

The two-part altar is about duality in its many forms, such as the divine aspects of duality, the duality of self, and the duality of relationships. We can also perceive a duality of the world—as above, so below—that can aid interaction with the angelic or faery realms.

The three-part altar brings variety and complexity, which can lead us through contemplation of divinity, the world around us, or particular qualities worth cultivating. It can also aid in decision making.

The four-part altar provides a way of examining the building blocks of our world: elements, directions, winds. The building blocks of who we are are also explored, as are ways to allow our true spirits to rise. In addition, basic principles by which we can live in balance with the mystical and practical can be found on this altar.

The way in which we interact with the world around us is explored in the five-part altar of the senses. However, like the other altar matrices, the five-part altar also offers explorations that range from personal qualities to the mythical and the mystical.

The six-part altar takes us through an exploration of movement and the sensation of taste. These intimate examinations allow us to develop genuine gratitude for the physical self. The balancing energy of the six-part altar can help us find unity between our higher and lower selves.

The seven-part altar brings us to the chakras. These are also related to the seven planets known to ancient astrologers. Even though seven is an odd number, the seven-pointed star matrix helps us find harmony and balance between the spiritual and physical. The seven-part altar also echoes the descent of Inanna with a meditation that allows us to descend into self to find the core of who we are.

The eight-part altar brings us outside ourselves with an exploration of moon cycles. The Eightfold Path of Buddhism and eight auspicious symbols provide for the contemplation of qualities that touch our lives on many levels.

Like the matrices before it, the nine-part altar takes us on explorations that lead us within and without with sacred woods, magic squares, and the Norse runes.

This book is meant to spark your imagination and to create personal adaptations that will allow you to access deeper meaning on your spiritual path. This book is also an interfaith exploration of the power in a personal altar as well as our relationship between self and the Divine. May your journey be rewarding.

The one thing that will never leave you,
once you transcend all unstable mental states,
is the joy of your soul.

—Paramahansa Yogananda

Altar Work

Meditation

Although considered by some to be a Buddhist practice, meditation is a tool used in many spiritual traditions. Texts found in 1945 at Nag Hammadi in Upper Egypt describe techniques of spiritual disciplines not unlike Buddhist or Hindu practices designed to achieve enlightenment.[1] Like the *Yoga Sutras* of Patanjali, the text called *Zostrianos* emphasized the importance of removing physical desires, reducing the chaos of the mind, and stilling it with meditation. Likewise, Paramahansa Yogananda called meditation "the science of being actively calm"[2] and considered daydreaming and sleeping to be forms of passive calmness.

Meditative pathways encompass a wide range of practices and spiritual orientations. The range includes koan meditation, vipassana, yoga, tai chi, ecstatic prayer, Hindu and Christian mysticism, the Western mystery schools, and the Kabbalah. In general terms, meditation has two primary facets: the search for the Divine and the search for the true or inner self. As these are frequently intertwined, it is common to seek the Divine in our everyday lives. Regardless of individual details, meditation is about one's spirituality and transformation.

---

1 Elaine Pagels, *The Gnostic Gospels*, 135.

2 Paramahansa Yogananda, *Inner Peace*, 19.

3

In a third-century province of Syria, spiritual master Yamliku (whose Latin name is Iamblichus) wrote a classic work called *On the Mysteries*. He emphasized a distinction between theology, what he called "talk about god," and theurgy, or "god work—doing the spiritual practices that actually produce real inner transformation."[3]

A question arises: how do we make this happen? The answer is that it will be slightly different for each person, and finding what works can be an interesting and rewarding journey. Whether it's concentrating on a symbol, rhythmical chanting, or physical movement, it comes down to focusing the mind. Over time, the mind becomes like a Möbius strip—a circle created by a strip of paper that has been twisted once before the ends are joined, so that the inner surface flows into the outer surface. In meditation, we move inward but eventually connect to the world outside, and vice versa.

This inward and outward flow occurs as we cultivate focus and mindfulness. Malcolm Eckel suggests the "deliberate cultivation of mental images."[4] In a commentary on Yoga Sutra 1:39, Pandit Rajmani Tigunait suggests that by meditating on an object of choice, one can attain "steadiness of mind." He also recommends that one use "wise selection" in the choice of objects on which to focus.[5] Using a series of objects or symbols creates a flowing meditation in which a "meditator works with a sequence of stimuli."[6] The stimuli become a chain of thoughts that lead deeper into the inner world toward insight (or "in-sight"), which is "seeing into the real nature of things."[7]

---

3 Linda Johnsen, "Beyond God Talk," 54–58.

4 Malcolm David Eckel, *Buddhism*, 60.

5 Pandit Rajmani Tigunait, "The Yoga Sutras," 52–53.

6 David Fontana, *The Meditator's Handbook*, 77.

7 Ibid., 57.

Grounding and Centering for Meditation

Sit comfortably and close your eyes so you can begin the shift from the everyday outer world to your interior space. Focus on your breathing, and let each breath start from your belly. Slowly fill your lungs, and then pause before you slowly exhale. The last air should leave from your belly. Pause again, and then start the next inhalation. Allow your body to let go of any tension. Become aware of your feet on the ground. Think of your energy extending below the floor, below the building to Mother Earth. Feel the solid foundation of earth that extends thousands of miles below you. The earth nourishes and cradles us.

Begin to draw this energy up into your body. Feel your legs become heavy and solid with earth energy. As you continue to draw the energy up into your abdomen—your center—feel the energy lighten into water. Continue to draw the energy up to your chest, to your heart, where we think of spirit and love. Feel the spark of fire energy burn there with the passion of life. As the energy continues upward, feel air energy, the power of mind and knowledge, surround your head. Hold the sensation of all four elements for a moment, and then allow the energy to return to Mother Earth, taking all negativity and tension from you.

Numbers: Sacred, Space, and Form

Since ancient times, people have had a desire to acknowledge numerical patterns in the world around them. This allows the mind to bring order to (or at least perceive it in) a seemingly chaotic universe and simplify a complicated world. For example, basic reckoning of time provided the means for mapping the cycles of the natural world. The ancient Sumerian, Babylonian, Chinese, Egyptian, Hindu, Celtic, Aztec, and Mayan people all developed complex calendar systems, which gave them the ability to make predictions—for example, when to sow seeds and when to prepare for weather changes or river flooding. In addition, numbers weren't just for counting days or predicting cycles; they were essential for making measurements and expressing abstract ideas. Even today, depending on the subject, a simple number can tell us if the weather is cold or hot (Fahrenheit or Celsius), the severity of an earthquake (Richter scale), the hardness of a crystal (Mohs scale), or the acidity or alkalinity of a substance (pH).

In ancient Greece, arithmetic was considered a high form of art since numbers were thought of as "abstract, spiritual entities."[8] Philosopher and mathematician Pythagoras (c. 560–480 BCE) held the belief that "the essence of everything seemed to be expressible in numbers."[9] He founded a school/community, part scientific and part religious, where he further developed his "theology of numbers": he believed that the study of arithmetic was the way to perfection.[10] Pythagoras ascribed symbolic meanings to numbers, which formed the basis for the practice of numerology. However, he wasn't the first. Numerology in one form or another was used by the Phoenicians, Hindus, Chinese, and Babylonians. The search for esoteric meaning in numbers was also pursued by the Sumerians and Egyptians, as well as the Aztecs and Maya. It seems that seeking metaphysical associations for patterns found in nature and attempting to understand the mysteries of life are basic human traits.

Gematria, the art of assigning numbers to letters, has been used to seek a connection between alphabets and numbers in the belief that a lost word of great power would be revealed. Gematria was used by the Babylonians in eighth century BCE,[11] as well as by medieval Kabbalists.[12] The Kabbalistic Tree of Life provides mystical interpretations of numbers, and the Enochian alphabet, with its numerical codes patterned into 644 lettered squares, was believed by John Dee and others to contain secret information.[13] True magic squares (grids of boxes with numbers whose sums are the same no matter which direction they are added) represented perfection and were used as amulets. The Sumerians believed that certain numbers

---

8 John McLeish, *Number*, 74–75.

9 Annemarie Schimmel, *The Mystery of Numbers*, 11.

10 John McLeish, *Number*, 51.

11 Annemarie Schimmel, *The Mystery of Numbers*, 34.

12 *Encyclopedia Britannica Micropaedia*, 15th ed., s.v. "Gematria."

13 David Allen Hulse, *The Western Mysteries*, 149.

represented particular gods and goddesses. Likewise, in the Bible, 666 is an example of a number that was believed to be a symbolic reference to a particular person; attempts to decipher it have challenged people throughout the centuries.[14] In many cultures and spiritual traditions, the notion of sacred numbers provides a way to deal with the great mysteries that confront us on a spiritual level. Numbers go beyond the function of symbols for the abstract; their use—mathematics—forms one of the building blocks that affect our experience of the physical world.

Pythagoras wasn't alone in associating numbers with shapes and exploring sacred geometry, where the relationship of form and proportion creates a vibrational resonance of interconnectedness. The ancient Chinese and Hindus designed temples with these harmonic principles, as did the builders of the great European cathedrals. Like sacred sites in nature, these places provide a setting in which to perceive and interact with divine energy.

Numbers are not just for measuring; when used symbolically, they can reveal underlying energy, purpose, pattern, and structure. According to Annemarie Schimmel, a number "develops a special character, a mystique of its own, and a special metaphysical meaning."[15] On an altar, they can serve as yantras—geometric diagrams for focusing the mind and accessing our numinous souls. As Patanjali pointed out in the *Yoga Sutras*, "Symbols should be used to help transcend them."[16] He also mentions that having a physical object or symbol helps the mind grasp abstract ideas and work with them on a deeper level. The altar grids in this book can also be perceived as geometric shapes, circles, and stars, which have transcendent qualities for the psyche to interact with them.

---

14 Annemarie Schimmel, *The Mystery of Numbers*, 277.

15 Ibid., 16.

16 Sri Swami Satchidananda, *The Yoga Sutras of Patanjali*, 123.

Methods: Who, Why, and How

In the introduction, I referred to the altar setups as "game boards" as an easy way to convey this idea. If you want to play backgammon you wouldn't use a chess board, as each board game has its own physical layout, its own rules, and its own mindset. However, using an altar matrix is no Candyland. It creates a place for serious contemplation and deepening of the soul. Dividing the altar top with specific intentions allows the mind to focus on a particular matrix of symbols in order to access certain energies. (Please note that the terms *matrix, layout, grid,* and *setup* are used interchangeably.)

Some altar setups in this book guide you through a sequence, while others provide room for your intuition to choose the path you need to follow around the altar top. Many setups are merely presented, allowing your personal intent to build the meditation sequence.

Overall, this book is an interfaith exploration of ourselves and our personal relationship with the Divine. While the concepts and practices presented here come from a variety of spiritual traditions, they do not require you to leave your own beliefs behind. We bring our own spirituality to the altar; it does not work the other way around.

This book is also about manifesting change in our lives. Some changes may be on the spiritual level while others are firmly rooted in the everyday world, but ultimately, because our lives do not consist of tidy pigeonholes, the mundane and sacred can flow throughout every aspect of life, bringing wholeness and balance.

Whether or not you use or keep a permanent altar, the altar layouts can help you focus your mind, open your energies, and receive information relevant to you at this point in your journey. These altar layouts can help you resolve issues or simply experience ideas in a new way. The altar matrix provides symbols or can be symbolic of ideas and energies. As symbols, the matrices provide the following:

- A way to access and activate archetypal energies

- A gateway to deeper layers of self

- A way to receive knowledge and wisdom

- Methods for aligning your physical, mental, and spiritual energies

- Alternative ways to view yourself and the world around you

- A system for working on life issues, big or small

Like yoga and other methods of using energy, altar matrices help us unlock emotions held within that we may have no other way to access. Since emotions and memories are not just in the mind but also in the body, you may find it helpful to do yoga or gentle stretching before settling in front of your altar.

Above all, the altar layout is a tool for accessing or processing knowledge. As such, you may find it useful to set up an altar grid that coincides with things in your life or with something you may be studying.

Like deep meditation, shamanic journeying, and vision quests, using an altar matrix consists of three steps for opening the self and accessing wisdom: symbol, trance, and vision, or concentration, tranquility, and insight, as noted by Dr. David Fontana.[17]

- Symbol/Concentration—A place to focus the mind; the altar

- Trance/Tranquility—Quiet the mind and allow it time to rest in stillness

- Vision/Insight—See what's there and be open to receive; *gnosis*

The first step, Symbol/Concentration, is the altar itself, which serves as a point of focus. The way in which you divide your altar and the things you place on it will serve as a pattern to access information and guidance.

The second step, Trance/Tranquility, does not mean that you have to put yourself into a hypnotic state. It is a matter of quieting the mind and letting go of the day-to-day chatter that clutters our heads. This step may take a little practice if you are not in the habit of meditating. Getting to this step is not difficult and only requires persistence and setting aside the time to allow yourself to get there. On the other hand, don't feel that

---

17 David Fontana, *The Meditator's Handbook*, 42.

you will need to reach a state of nirvana in order to make it work. Simply be present in the moment as you focus on the symbols on your altar.

In the third step, Vision/Insight, meditation and contemplation begin with intention, but once the altar is set up and you sit before it, all intention must be set aside, because our minds can interpret intention to mean expectation. If we don't hear a choir of angels and zoom right to a higher level, we may be disappointed and give up. This is a product of our modern world: we expect gratification instantly. However, true change comes in its own time. Whether from within or from outside, wisdom comes softly into our consciousness. It may arrive as an image if you are a visually oriented person, or it may come as a feeling or something that you "just know." The important point is to be open to receive. Information may come to you as you sit in front of your altar or it may come later—even a day or two later. It may also happen over time if you repeat your work with a particular altar grid. You may find that you need to make adjustments in the altar setup as you continue to work with it. Remain open to your intuition and allow it to guide you.

The main requirement for working with layouts is that your altar be located where you can sit comfortably in front of it. If you have a permanent altar that is located on a shelf, you may want to use a temporary altar on a table that has sufficient space. If your altar shares a desk or table with other things, consider covering the everyday items with a tablecloth or towel, or firmly set a mental demarcation between these things and your altar area.

The way in which you physically set up your altar matrix is a personal decision that depends on how you prefer to work. If it is best for you to physically divide the space on the top of your altar into sections, do so. This can be done by using a large piece of paper and simply drawing a grid for whichever altar matrix you plan to use. For example, if you are using a nine-part altar matrix, it would look like a tick-tack-toe grid. If you are doing a four-part element or direction matrix, you could use different pieces of construction paper that correspond to the colors associated with these according to your tradition or practice. If you prefer to work a little more simply, you can use anything straight and thin to demarcate the borders of the sectors. Items such as pencils, twigs, and chopsticks work well, as do cut lengths of string. Each sector does not need to be completely walled off. Experiment to see what works for you.

Once you have used an altar matrix, you may find it useful to leave it in place for a day or two or longer. The power of your intention and energy raised may help to propel you along the path of study or energy work. Seeing a particular setup frequently after meditating with it may serve as a gentle reminder for you. Leaving the altar matrix in place also allows it to evolve, as you may find yourself adding to it as you continue to ponder and work with the experience. This is especially helpful if it is a meditation you intend to repeat.

After a time, if you find that a particular altar matrix is important to you, you may want to make it more permanent. This could be done by creating a special altar cloth by stitching different colors of cloth together or by drawing a grid with fabric paint. Alternatively, a piece of wood or foam board could be painted to suit your purpose. These could be kept under an altar cloth that you remove when you want to use the matrix. However, in working with symbols, Patanjali noted that we should use them as spiritual aids but be prepared to outgrow them and move on. Once you have learned the necessary lesson for you within an altar matrix, move on to a new one or expand on it in such a way that you are able to continue to grow. I find that the three-part matrix is a powerful setup for me, but the content evolves. Alternatively, you may find it beneficial to repeat an altar matrix meditation without using the physical altar setup. The sacred space you create with an altar and your intent may hold the energy of the matrix after it has been disassembled. Follow your intuition and experiment.

While setting up the altar matrix, use the time for mental preparation with silence or perhaps soothing music, saying or singing chants that will help you to transition away from your everyday mindset. When the altar is ready, seat yourself comfortably in front of it. Close your eyes and continue singing or chanting, or quietly focus your attention on your breath until you feel relaxed and calm. The present moment is the only thing you need to be aware of; yesterday is over and tomorrow does not yet exist. Anything important will return to your mind when you have finished the meditation; if it doesn't, then it wasn't truly important.

Another way to begin is to become aware of your feet on the floor. If you are sitting on the floor, become aware of your "sit bones" in contact with the floor (or pillow). Think of your energy as extending downward through the floor, through the building to the foundation and below to the earth. Sense your connection with Mother Earth, with the natural world, and with the universe. Feel your place on this planet and, in turn, its place in the cosmos. The energy of the universe is the same energy that flows through you. Slowly bring your awareness back to your inner world. When you feel connected and centered, open your eyes to a soft gaze and begin the meditation. Guidance on how to proceed is provided in each altar section.

During meditation when other thoughts intrude, acknowledge them and then set them aside. Remind yourself that if they are important then they will come back to you later. Trying to push thoughts away, ignore them, or set up a barrier in the belief that they won't intrude may provide more of a distraction than the distracting thought. If you find that you have become distracted, don't beat yourself up about it. Be glad that part of your mind has realized the distraction. Simply accept it and return to where you were. Despite interruptions from our chattering monkey brains, if we can stay focused and keep returning to the point of focus, the meditation will move deeper and we will be able to peel back each layer of onion skin toward our inner core, our real nature.

When you conclude a meditation, take time to ponder the experience. Let it touch you deeply. Take the knowledge into your soul so it becomes part of you. You may find it useful to journal your experience. Impressions can fade quickly, and by recording information, you will be able to return to it later to pick up threads that can help you weave your pattern of growth. Above all, trust your intuition to guide you.

The
One-Part Altar

The Number One

As a symbol of unity and wholeness, the number one represents the universe and everything interconnected into one entity. One can be alone (all one) or only (one-like), whereas union, universe, and university represent many as one.[1]

One is considered magic because from nothing (null, zero) comes one. From the primordial void came the universe. One is the creative force from which all things flow. In the creation myths of China and Japan, the universe began as a primordial cosmic egg. This is a concept shared by the Old European, Minoan, and Maltese cultures.

On the other hand, one comes from two: from sperm and egg, a new life is created, and during an eclipse, the sun and moon are seen to join as one. If you work with a two-part altar representing Goddess and God, you may want to come back to the one-part setup and meditate on the Divine Child, Mabon, Jesus, or Holy Spirit.

Hermetic alchemists associated the number one with the philosopher's stone, an essential ingredient in the transmutation of any metal into silver or gold.[2] The number one represents a standing person—life force. One also represents beginnings and manifestation. The Egyptian sun god Re

---

1 John H. Conway and Richard K. Guy, *The Book of Numbers*, 3.

2 Ibid., 4.

was sometimes called "the one One." Neter was the formless god who preceded all others. In monotheistic faiths, God is the One and the intent or mystical practice is to lose one's separate identity and merge with the One.[3]

Basic Associations

beginnings	fertility	primacy
the center	first	source
contemplation	focus	unity
creativity	individual	wholeness
the Divine (supreme	isolation	will
Goddess or God)	light	
ego	manifestation	

Using the One-Part Altar

Something from Nothing: The Void of Creation

The concept of nothingness can be overwhelming. Working with the one-part altar can be a challenge, but as previously mentioned, the evolution of something from nothing is a major event. You may want to begin with a completely empty altar. Assess how you feel with this emptiness. Do you get a sense of spaciousness, as though your mind could expand and become part of all that is?

As a symbol of humankind being the only creature to walk upright (1 = I), be mindful to not let the ego get out of balance. Instead of focusing on *numero uno*, you can think in terms of your being part of the "One"—part of all that exists.

If you choose to work with no symbolic object, the emptiness can represent the endless void of space. Or it could represent a womb—empty, but ready to receive and then create. To the people of Neolithic Europe, tombs were also considered symbolic of the womb of the Great Mother

---

3 Annemarie Schimmel, *The Mystery of Numbers*, 44.

Goddess. Death was associated with rebirth, and tombs were frequently places of ritual.[4] To enter the tomb was symbolic of surrendering one's self as one returned to the belly of Mother Earth. Re-emerging after ritual was symbolic of rebirth, resurrection, and renewal.

You may consider setting your intention for a blank altar to be a clean slate upon which will be written a new phase of your life or some aspect in which you seek change. The emptiness can represent purity—a new part of you that is not corrupted by outside judgment or opinion. It may be a step in finding or creating an aspect of you that is ready to be manifested—birthed into existence. Acknowledge the beginning of something new in your life: new challenges, new opportunities, new situations, or a different phase of life. Celebrate the birth of a child or acknowledge you are becoming an elder—a sage or crone.

If you usually have a cloth with a design covering your altar, you may want to try using the bare altar top or a single-colored cloth. The color of the cloth can be a symbol itself. Without an object on the altar, focus on the color and allow your mind to work with it for meaningful associations. Table 1.1 contains a list of colors and corresponding attributes. Alternatively, use what you have at hand and allow the randomness to guide your meditation.

The Well: Primal Source

Another way to work with the blank altar is to look down at it as though you are looking into a well. It can represent an empty well waiting for the rains of inspiration or a well of wisdom like Connla's Well in Celtic mythology or Mimir's Well in Norse legend.[5] Connla's Well was the source of inspiration and knowledge for anyone who partook of the water in it or ate a salmon from its waters. Perhaps a blue altar cloth can represent your soul's well and be the source of knowledge for you. Go back to your own source. Finding your inner child may serve to bring you to the essence of

---

4 Marija Gimbutas, *The Language of the Goddess*, 223.

5 James MacKillop, *Dictionary of Celtic Mythology*, 103.

TABLE 1.1—ATTRIBUTES AND ASSOCIATIONS OF BASIC COLORS

Color	Meaning
Black	Class, depth, elegance, mourning, mystery, primordial void, power, protection, sophistication, style
Blue	Calm, confidence, devotion, harmony, healing, honesty, intuition, integrity, knowledge, loyalty, patience, peace, self-awareness, sincerity, stability, tranquility, truth
Brown	Abundance, balance, comfort, groundedness, hearth, home, simplicity, stability
Gray	Dignity, intelligence, maturity, security, serenity, reliability
Green	Abundance, adaptability, balance, fertility, growth, health and healing, immortality, luck, nature, prosperity, renewal, vigor, youth
Orange	Action, adaptability, change, creativity, energy, justice, kindness, pleasure, receptivity, success, warmth, zest
Pink	Beauty, gentleness, grace, emotions, fidelity, health, honor, hope, inner child, innocence, love, morality, rest, romance
Purple	Authority, communication with the Divine, enchantment, healing, idealism, independence, nobility, power, royalty, spirituality, transformation, wisdom
Red	Courage, creative energy, desire, emotions, excitement, fertility, health, imagination, love, passion, power, respect, strength, unity, willpower
White	Balance, cleanliness, clairvoyance, enlightenment, faith, goodness, healing, highest consciousness, hope, innocence, peace, perfection, protection, purity, reverence, sacredness, secrecy, simplicity, truth
Yellow	Clarity, communication, confidence, friendship, happiness, hope, intellect, joy, knowledge, psychic awareness, unity

who you are. Going inward (sometimes toward darkness) can help you find your inner light.

A single object in the center of your altar can be a powerful point of focus. The object you use can represent the purpose of your meditation. For example, if connecting with the Divine is your intent, a photograph, statue, or symbol of your worship, such as a spiral or cross, can be the object of focus. If you are working with the concept of a well, experiment with the hexagram of the Well from the *I Ching* (Book of Changes). The

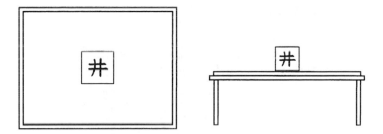

Figure 1.1—The Well hexagram can be used
flat on the altar or standing up for easier viewing.

Chinese *kanji* character used in this hexagram resembles the pound sign
(#)[6] and represents a method for drawing upon the deep strength within
the mystery of life. In ancient Greece, the Eleusinian Mysteries acknowledged the divine spark from which life was created and which lies within
the deepest part (the well) of our souls. The Well is a symbol of reaching
deep inside oneself to connect with one's own energy, which is necessary
in order to connect with one's true self.

Paint or draw the Well symbol on a piece of paper and place it in the
center of your altar. Let it lie flat if you are going to look down at the altar; otherwise, fold the card in half so it will stand up and you can see it
as you sit.

A less obvious object can sometimes function better, since preconceived
icons can potentially inhibit the reception of other images or impressions.
Candles, crystals, and gemstones work well in this regard. Like the altar
cloth, a candle can symbolize your intention by its color. A crystal or gemstone has vibrational attributes that can further enhance your meditation.
Table 1.2 provides a basic guide to the colors and attributes of common
gemstones.

If you use a crystal or gemstone that you have worked with before,
it may already be imbued with your intent. If it is a new stone or you
have used it for other purposes, you may want to cleanse it first. (Refer to

---

6 Johndennis Govert, *Feng Shui*, 9.

TABLE 1.2—GEMSTONE COLORS AND ATTRIBUTES

Gemstone	Colors	Attributes
Agate	Blue, gray, green, pink, white	General healer; good for grounding and balance; aids in attracting abundance and luck; promotes longevity and strength; provides protection
Amber	Red-brown, yellow	General healer; good for balance and calming; associated with wisdom and knowledge
Amethyst	Purple	General healer (physical and spiritual); calms and transforms
Apatite	Green, pink, purple, white, yellow	Promotes concentration; aids the intellect; promotes harmony
Aquamarine	Blue, green, white	Produces mental clarity; aids in dealing with loss, grief, and fear
Aventurine	Green	General healer; enhances success in career; aids creativity
Azurite	Blue	For cleansing and spiritual guidance; promotes patience
Beryl	Blue, green, pink, red, white, yellow	Stimulates communication and acceptance
Bloodstone	Green, red	Attracts good luck and abundance
Carnelian	Red	Aids creativity and self-worth
Chalcedony	Black, blue, gray, red, white, yellow	Alleviates melancholy; builds vitality
Chrysoberyl	Blue, green, purple, yellow	Fosters benevolence and optimism
Citrine	Yellow	Boosts creativity and self-worth; attracts prosperity and stability; aids protection
Coral	Black, pink, red, white	Clears negativity; stimulates relationships; provides protection
Diamond	Black, blue, pink, white, yellow	Builds relationships; attracts abundance; supports longevity
Emerald	Green	Provides insight; a healer that helps navigate difficulties
Fluorite	Blue, green, purple, red, white, yellow	Provides protection and strength in times of transition
Garnet	Green, purple	Promotes confidence and success

Gemstone	Colors	Attributes
Jade	Green, purple, white	General healer; promotes longevity and wisdom
Jet	Black	Engenders honor and justice; provides protection during transitions
Lapis lazuli	Blue	Promotes inner power and tranquility; expands understanding
Malachite	Green	Attracts loyalty and comfort; aids in navigating setbacks and difficulties
Moonstone	Gray, white	Alleviates fear; balances yin and yang; promotes protection through insight
Obsidian	Black	Provides grounding and insight; dispels half-truths
Onyx	Black, white	Helps control emotions and negative thoughts
Opal	Black, blue, green, red, white	Stimulates a wider vision
Pearl	Black, gray, white	Induces emotional balance and openness
Peridot	Green	General healing, especially hurt feelings; attracts comfort; builds vitality
Quartz	Black, blue, gray, green, pink, purple, white	General healing and balancing—emotional and physical; alleviates anger; reveals distortion
Ruby	Red	Strengthens self-esteem and integrity; attracts and engenders generosity; dispels fear
Sapphire	Blue, green, pink, purple, red, white, yellow	Promotes mental clarity and intuition
Spinel	Blue, green, pink, purple, red, white	General healer; enhances ability to overcome obstacles and setbacks; enhances communication
Topaz	Blue, green, pink, red, yellow	Alleviates tension; promotes communication; attracts abundance
Tourmaline	Black, blue, green, pink, purple, red, white, yellow	Aids in dealing with grief; dispels fear for positive change; provides protection from negative energy
Turquoise	Blue, green	General healing; protects against negativity
Zircon	Blue, green, purple, red, white, yellow	Attracts prosperity and abundance

Appendix B for information on cleansing methods.) You do not have to stick with polished gems or intricate crystals. Uncut gemstones that have not been tumbled or worked can be very attractive. Likewise, a stone that you found on a walk through the woods or along a beach can be just as potent. Let your intuition guide you for what is appropriate for your altar.

Pyramid Power

In addition to focusing on the symbolic meaning of the object, it can also be used to evoke the power of a pyramid or create a "cone of power"[7] on the altar top—think three-dimensional. Pyramid energy is associated with higher spiritual desires, and if this is what you are striving for, try working with this concept. Pyramid energy or a cone of power can help raise and project your intentions into the world. When you set up your altar, align one side to the north; use a compass to determine magnetic north so that each side is aligned to the cardinal directions, which will enhance the energy. Using an object on the altar can help you visualize the pyramid. A crystal or gemstone placed in the center is particularly effective for this. Not only will the stone help you visualize the pyramid, but its energy will be amplified.

Stay with the energy as long as it does not become a distraction from your meditation. When the meditation has run its course, allow the energy to dissolve and be sure to ground your personal energy. (Refer to "Altar Work" earlier in the book for information on grounding and centering.)

Solar Plexus: Solar Deity

If your altar is a low table, you may want to begin by visualizing energy moving from the crystal or other object to your solar plexus and then back to the altar. Connecting center to center will help to bring you to center and into yourself. In ancient India, it was believed that the soul and body were joined at the solar plexus. The solar plexus chakra is called the *Ma-*

---

7 Starhawk, *The Spiral Dance*, 146.

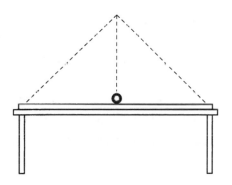

Figure 1.2—An object in the center of the altar aids in
defining where the peak of the pyramid or cone should rise.

nipura, which means "the seat of the soul." It is the seat of our instincts,
which are sometimes called our animal soul, and it is a source for inner
guidance. (Refer to "The Seven-Part Altar" for more information on the
chakras.)

As you settle in front of your altar, prepare for meditation as you normally do. To build the energy in your solar plexus, slowly chant "RAM"
(pronounced "RUM"[8]), the chakra's seed sound, three times as you visualize your intent. When you feel the energy in your stomach area, chant
"AH" to move and release the energy. Feel it move from your solar plexus,
your inner sun, and connect with the gemstone or other object on your
altar. As this connection strengthens, begin to visualize the sides of the
pyramid forming. Let the interior of this energy pyramid begin to fill with
your intention. Hold it for as long as you can and then let it dissolve.
(Also refer to the next section, which deals with pulling energy.)

To emphasize a solar connection, you may want to use a piece of amber,
citrine, golden topaz, or any object that is gold or representative of the sun.
Let the energy move from your solar plexus to the object. Instead of visualizing a pyramid, imagine a cord of energy continuing from your altar to

---

8 An easy way to remember the seed sound for the solar plexus chakra is to think of the
warming sensation of rum in the stomach.

the sun itself. Think of your intention being boosted by the power of this day star and radiating out to the universe. Just as light and energy radiates outward, it is also reflected back. Allow the return of energy to move you deeper into your meditation.

To enhance the movement of energy, consider chanting the name of one or several solar deities or using one of their images as the focal object on the altar. Table 1.3 lists the names of gods and goddesses associated with the sun.

Projecting and Pulling Energy

A square, rectangular, or round altar table works well for the above suggestions, with the square being the best for the pyramid. The following suggestions, however, are ideal for a triangular-shaped table, which can be used to amplify the energy you send out or to direct energy toward you. If a triangular-shaped table is not available, creating this shape on your current altar can function just as well, because your intent will be to ignore the blocked-out areas. Ideally, the parts of the altar top that will be outside the triangle should be a dark color in order to create a background for the triangle and make it easier to distinguish. If your altar is not a dark color, place a plain dark cloth over the top. Draw and then cut out a triangle from a large piece of paper or tape several sheets of paper together to get the right size. The color of the triangle should be lighter than the background; however, you can coordinate its color with the intent of your purpose.

If your intent is to project or release energy (symbolic of releasing something from your life), sit in front of your altar with the wide end of the triangle toward you. Once you settle into your breath, shift your awareness to your energy field. Similar to the method for the solar connection's movement of energy, focus your attention on your heart center instead of your solar plexus.

TABLE 1.3—SUN GODS AND GODDESSES

Name	Cultural association
Ah Kin	Mayan
Ahau-Kin	Mayan
Amateratsu	Japan/Shinto
Anhur/Anhert	Egypt
Apollo	Roman
Atum/Aten	Egypt
Bel/Belinos/Belenus	Celtic
Cautha	Etruscan
Etain	Celtic
Frey	Norse
Helios	Greek
Horus	Egypt
Hitzilopochtli	Aztec
Inti	Inca
Janus/Giano	Etruscan
Lugh	Celtic/Irish
Manco	Inca
Mithra	Persia
Ra/Re	Egypt
Shamash/Sama	Babylonian
Sol	Roman
Surya	Hindu
Tonatiuh	Aztec
Utu	Sumerian

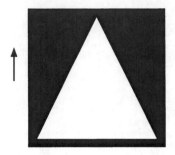

Figure 1.3—Projecting or releasing energy and intention.
Sit with the point of the triangle facing away from you.

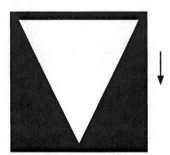

Figure 1.4—Pulling energy.
Sit with the point of the triangle facing toward you.

To build the energy in your heart center, slowly chant "YAM" (pro-nounced "YUM"[9]), the chakra's seed sound, three times as you visualize your intent. When you feel the energy in your heart area, chant "AY" to move and release the energy. Feel it move from your body and gather speed as it crosses the triangle and then becomes focused as it reaches the point and goes out to the universe to fulfill your purpose.

When your intention is to attract things into your life, sit on the op-posite side of your altar, with the point of the triangle facing toward you.

---

9 An easy way to remember the seed sound for the heart chakra is to think of a life with love as being yummy.

Prepare yourself in the same way, but instead of releasing energy, think of opening your heart center to receive. As you do this, visualize what you want to bring into your life. This is especially helpful in drawing healing energy. Visualize the energy coming to you and going to the place that needs healing.

In addition to opening the heart center when pulling energy, also engage the solar plexus chakra. The symbol of the Manipura chakra is a downward-pointing triangle, which represents power moving from the universe to you. Trust kindled by courage (solar plexus chakra) and compassion (heart chakra) support you to live in truth.

List of Correspondences for the Number One

Astrology: Aries, Mars, Mercury, Sun, Uranus

Colors: Gold, orange, red, white, yellow

Day of the week: Sunday

Element: Fire

Energy: Masculine and feminine

Gemstones: Diamond, garnet, ruby

Message: "I am"

Months: January, October

Pythagorean name: Monad

Rune: Ansuz

Tarot: The Magician

The
Two-Part Altar

The Number Two

Two, the only even prime number, represents anything of a binary nature: light/dark, sun/moon, male/female, goddess/god, yin/yang, active/passive, good/evil. Two illustrates that everything is dualistic and has another side that may not always be visible. It represents the "descent of spirit into matter."[1]

Two can represent contrast and division—a breaking apart of the primordial one—as well as reflection and stability. Something with two sides can be naturally balanced. Opposites that attract can unify and come into balance.

Two signifies a doubling, which is usually considered a good thing. Two heads are better than one; a pair has twofold wisdom or strength. Two represents a relationship. For Christians, two became associated with the male godhead: God the Father and Christ the Son. It also represents the dual nature of Jesus: human and divine.

Two has also been seen as discordant for strict monotheists because of the belief that there is only one god. For this reason, Agrippa of Nettesheim declared two "the number of man" who is separate from the Divine.[2]

---

1 John H. Conway and Richard K. Guy, *The Book of Numbers*, 57.
2 Annemarie Schimmel, *The Mystery of Numbers*, 47.

TABLE 2.1—DUALITY AND COMPLEMENTARY RELATIONSHIPS

Male	Female
God	Goddess
Sun	Moon
Christ the Son	God the Father
Jesus	Mary
Divine Son/Mabon	Goddess/Modron
Mind	Body
Yang	Yin
Motion	Rest
Left	Right
Divine	Human

TABLE 2.2—DUALITY PRESENTS CHOICE

Either	Or
Push	Pull
In	Out
Up	Down
Sweet	Savory
Hot	Cold
Straight	Curved

Two can also represent choice. When we have only one of something, that's it—take it or leave it. Two brings a different dynamic: You can have this or that. You can go in or out.

Hatha yoga is a discipline for working with the polarity of energies. *Ha* means "sun" and *tha* means "moon."[3] The solar plexus is the inner sun, and the inner moon is at the base of the spine. The balancing of these chakras and energies allows one to reach one's higher potential. The male and female energies intertwine around each other in a dance as old as time. Female energy travels up a channel called the *ida*, which begins and ends on the right side of the body. Male energy travels up the *pingala*, which begins and ends on the left.[4]

Many English words containing *tw* are associated with two: *twice, twin, twain, between, betwixt, twilight, twist/twill* (two threads together), and, of course, *two* itself. *Dual, duel,* and *duet* are also associated with two.[5]

---

3 Sri Swami Satchidananda, *The Yoga Sutras of Patanjali*, 58.

4 Anodea Judith, *Wheels of Life*, 36–40.

5 John H. Conway and Richard K. Guy, *The Book of Numbers*, 4–5.

Basic Associations

balance	love	sexuality
duality	opposites	solidarity
division	partnership	stillness
harmony	polarity	tolerance
healing	separation	

Using the Two-Part Altar

Divine Aspects of Duality

A common configuration for Neopagan altars emphasizes the duality and unity of Goddess and God by dividing it in half and assigning each deity and its attributes a side. Whether following the lead of Indian yogis or responding to the natural force of our bodies, many Pagans assign the right side of the altar to the Goddess and the left to the God. However, if your tradition tells you otherwise, you should continue your custom and follow what is comfortable for you.

Working with this setup allows you to honor both Goddess and God on equal terms. Table 2.3 lists God/Goddess couples along with their symbols, which can be used or represented on your altar. This list is offered as a sample, as there are many others. It is common in some Pagan rituals to pair up deities regardless of whether or not they appear together in myth or cultural history. If you have a special affinity for a particular set of Goddess and God even though they are not a divine couple, follow your heart of hearts to tell you whether their combined energy provides balance for you. This altar setup can also be instrumental in balancing one's male and female energies. (Also refer to the Three-Part Altar.)

While a divided altar top emphasizes difference, it also signifies unity: the two parts complement each other and come together in union. In mythology, the unity of Goddess and God produces the Divine Child, the Mabon. For Christians, the dual altar can represent God and Christ or the Madonna and Child. This altar setup is also a powerful tool for prayer.

TABLE 2.3—GODS AND GODDESSES AND THEIR RELATED SYMBOLS

God	Goddess	Culture
Adonis—plants, myrrh, boar	Aphrodite [Venus]—apple, dove, myrtle tree, rose, swan	Greek [Roman]
Balder—mistletoe	Nanna—earth	Norse
Bíle [Beli]—oak tree	Danu/Dana [Dôn]—water	Celtic Ireland [Wales]
Brahma—lotus, swan, water	Savaswathi—swan, peacock, book	Hindu
Dagda—cauldron, harp, staff	Boann—water, hazelnuts, white cow	Celtic Ireland
Dumuzi [Tammuz]—plants, cedar trees, bull	Inanna [Ishtar]—crescent waning moon, eight-pointed star	Sumerian [Babylonian]
Horus—hawk, eye	Hathor—cow, sun disk flanked by horns, turquoise	Egyptian
Pwyll (1st)—white stag Manawydan (2nd)—seashells, swine	Rhiannon—birds, horse	Celtic Wales
Odin/Wodin—ash tree, raven, runes	Frigg—spindle (wool for spinning), stars (Orion constellation/Friggjar)	Norse
Osiris—pillar, sycamore tree, feathers, barley	Isis—moon, sun disk flanked by cow horns	Egyptian
Shiva—lingam, crescent moon	Parvati/Sakthi—blue lotus	Hindu
Tegrid Foel—water, boar	Cerridwen—cauldron, boar, moon, salmon	Celtic Wales
Thor—thunderbolt, wheel, goat	Sif—gold	Norse
Vishnu—conch shell, lotus	Lakshmi—coins, grain	Hindu
Zeus [Jupiter]—eagle, oak, thunderbolt	Hera [Juno]—cow, peacock, pomegranate	Greek [Roman]

Square brackets ([ ]) show the equivalent name in the culture indicated.

34

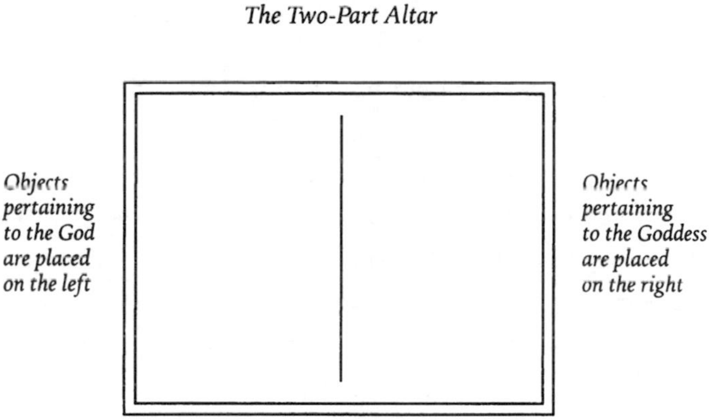

Figure 2.1—The two-part setup emphasizes duality.

Duality and Self

Because of its binary nature, two can be used to emphasize division as well as harmony. Acknowledging a difference or separation can be the catalyst for healing. Sometimes in a close relationship or partnership the individual can lose his or her identity, making it important to acknowledge being a separate individual as well as part of a couple.

When working with the self, taking time to look both inward and outward brings balance. The rational (scientific, factual knowledge) and the transrational (myth, poetry, artistic inspiration) can be reconciled and co-exist—after all, these represent the two halves of our brains. Similarly, most people are not made up of exclusively male or female energy, and it can be very healing to acknowledge and honor all that is the self. Polarities can create power that is neither one nor the other but a joining of the two: we are a blend of two primal energies.

In many cases, when we examine differences and divisions in order to produce change and transformation, we frequently find that we must go through a difficult process. Many times, there are minor aspects that need change, but occasionally we need to take the bull by the horns and deal with major issues of the self. When we disrupt things in our lives, we find that they begin to rupture and break apart. In essence, we begin to break open—to hatch. This can be a scary prospect, because it requires us to leave our comfort zone and bring our naked, vulnerable inner self out into the glare of the scrutiny of the outer self.

Some small part of our minds might actually rebel and ask, "What's the point of all this?" because part of us likes the safety of routine and sameness. The more important the change, the scarier it can be. This is the core of many myths and fairy tales: the little guy (inner self) is pushed out into the big, cruel world (outer self) to face the dangerous dragon/witch/troll/giant (something that holds us back from our full potential). However, once we face division—the tearing apart—we can begin to truly heal, grow, and come into our true self. We can morph from a caterpillar into a butterfly.

A two-part altar can help you focus intention and manifest change. The general flow of energy coming to and leaving us goes from left to right. Place objects on the left half of your altar to symbolize what you want to invite into your life. On the right, place things that symbolize what you want to release. Instead of physical objects, you may find it more appropriate to write a few keywords on small pieces of paper that you place on the respective sides of the altar top. Putting feelings into words can be an empowering process, and you may want to write a full description of your situation; alternatively, place this description on your altar.

Another technique is to use two candles. The colors can be relevant to what you are releasing and drawing into your life, or you can use one color and scratch your keywords into the wax. Place the candles on their respective sides of the altar.

Once you have set up your altar, prepare as you would for any meditation. If you are using candles, light the one on the right side. When your breath is relaxed and you feel calm, begin to visualize what you want to release or change. Let emotions come to the surface, and then visualize them as bubbles floating off from the right side of your altar as well as from your body. Take time with this even if it is painful, because it will be a cleansing process. Remove the unwanted and let it go. As it departs, it makes room for something else. If this is an emotional exercise for you, you may feel emptiness inside. Allow yourself to experience this sensa-

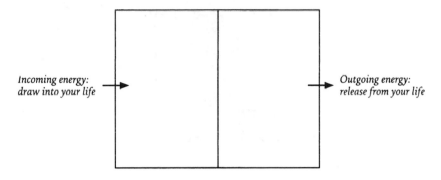

Incoming energy:
draw into your life

Outgoing energy:
release from your life

Figure 2.2—Manifesting intentions. Energy moves through us from left to right.

tion: you are an empty vessel that has been washed clean and is open to receive. Extinguish the candles if you are using them.

Continue to hold this feeling of emptiness for a few moments or as long as it feels appropriate. When you are ready, if you are using candles, light the one on the left side of the altar as you begin to focus your attention on what you want to draw into your life. Visualize the change it may bring. Spend time with any thoughts and images that may arise. When you feel comfortable, remove any objects that you placed on the right side of your altar. Remove whatever you used to mark the division of the altar top, and place any objects from the left side in the middle. Continue to hold your thoughts or images of the changes you invited into your life. When it feels appropriate, end your meditation. You may find it useful to journal your experience so you can refer to it as you progress.

If you want a more visual cue for the movement of energy, you may want to try a technique mentioned in "The One-Part Altar." Cut out two triangles from a large piece of white or light-colored art paper to block out sections of your altar. If your altar is a light color, place a dark cloth over it before laying out the triangles. The triangles could also be defined by arranging four sticks of fairly equal size so that they radiate out from the center to each corner. One stick can be used to create a simple division.

If you feel a particular affinity with trees, you could coordinate the type of tree branches with the type of issue with which you are dealing.

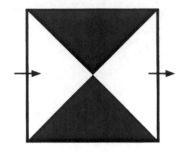

Figure 2.3—Visible cues help visualize the movement of energy.

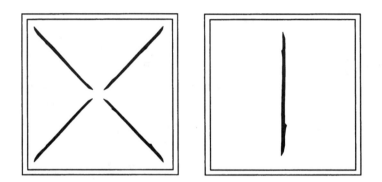

Figure 2.4—Sticks can be used to create the triangles or a simple division of space.

For example, if it has to do with summoning strength to make changes in your life, oak would be a good tree to use. If it is healing you seek, maple or hawthorn could add the energy you need. Table 2.4 contains a brief list of common trees and their associated energies. Other trees and their associations can be found in Table 9.1 of "The Nine-Part Altar."

Duality in Relationships

I am sure that I don't really need to mention how challenging a relationship can be. Whether it is with a parent, sibling, spouse/partner, friend, or colleague, a relationship takes care and attention. Otherwise, it withers and dies or becomes a nebulous wall between two people that causes indifference.

TABLE 2.4—ATTRIBUTES AND ENERGIES OF TREES

Tree	Associated energies
Cedar	Balance, healing, prosperity, wisdom
Cherry	Achievement, action, joy, playfulness
Chestnut	Healing, love, prosperity
Hackberry	Adaptability, creativity
Hickory	Abundance, flexibility, generosity
Juniper	Cleansing, healing, love
Magnolia	Clarity, self-awareness, truth
Locust	Balance, friendship, perseverance, strength
Maple	Abundance, grounding, transformation, wisdom
Mimosa	Happiness, love, peace, sensitivity
Myrtle	Fertility, healing, love, luck, peace
Palm	Abundance, fertility, potency, strength
Spruce	Enlightenment, grounding, intuition, well-being
Sycamore	Communication, shelter, vitality
Witch hazel	Healing, inspiration, protection

In many cases when we need to confront issues with other people, we should start with ourselves in order to get our own energies aligned with the task ahead. Sometimes if we just mentally go through the steps we need to take and visualize the movement of energy, we can begin the process of change. To do this, set up your altar top with a double triangle as described above.

For this work, place the triangles so that you can sit facing the wide side of one of them. Prepare yourself as you would for meditation. When you are comfortable and ready, imagine the other person sitting on the opposite side with the wide side of the other triangle in front of them. In your mind, go through the steps or actions you feel are necessary for both of you to resolve the issue. Even if you feel that the other person is stubborn and would not take these steps, think of it happening. As you do

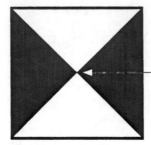

*Common ground;
point of balance
and agreement*

Your seated position

Figure 2.5—The relationship grid can help
manifest balancing energies between people.

this, visualize your energies coming together to resolve the issue. Placing an object that symbolizes the resolution as the fulcrum of the triangles can enhance the process.

If it is a particularly difficult problem, you may need to go through this a number of times before actually dealing with the person face to face. Going through this process on your own first can help you find solutions as well as prepare you to be a calm influence on the situation.

This method is not limited to big issues in your relationships, and if the other person also engages in meditation or ritual, you may be able to make this a shared experience. You will need to explain the process ahead of time and both be willing to relate your visualizations as they progress. Be sure you have enough room for both of you to sit comfortably on opposite sides of the altar.

Above and Below

Numerous cultures—past and present—carry a belief in the existence of other beings inhabiting nearby realms and sometimes the human plane. In our own twenty-first-century culture, it is not unusual to call on saints, deities, angels, and faeries for help. This is done through prayer, meditation, and shamanic journeying. Whatever your method, setting an altar to pattern the energies can assist you. Your altar can be as elaborate or

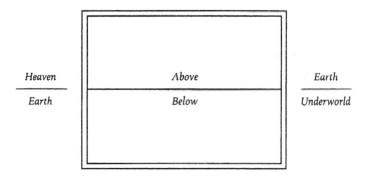

Heaven / Earth   Above / Below   Earth / Underworld

Figure 2.6—The realms altar.

simple as you like. Use many objects or none except for the dividing line, which will be horizontal to where you sit.

If you seek the help of angels, saints, and heavenly deities, visualize the altar halves as heaven and earth. If you seek the faeries and chthonic deities, visualize the earth and underworld realms.

With this altar setup, you can use a complete visualization process, meditate with your mind open to receive information, or simply sit and gaze upon objects placed in the sections. In place of objects, you can write the name of a saint or deity on a piece of paper and place it on the appropriate half of the altar. Write your own name or the name of another person for whom you may be seeking something, such as healing, on the other side. If you have worked with angels or faeries and know one of their individual names, write that on a slip of paper, or simply write "Angels" or "Faeries."

Yahweh, Buddha, Christ, Vedic deities, and the Greek Olympians represent the shining, luminous gods and goddesses to which humans have aspired for millennia. They are thought of as occupying the heavenly realms. While a number of Pagan gods and goddesses are associated with the sun or moon, for the most part they occupy the earthly realm.

The deities of the underworld seem to exist in a deep, shadowy place that many have been taught to fear. However, unlike the notion of a hell filled with eternal torment, underworld deities serve to balance their heavenly counterparts. These chthonic gods and goddesses offer rest, renewal, and guidance. Just as we in the darkness of our mothers' wombs find our beginnings, those who journey into the underworld find rebirth. Just as the Celtic bards of centuries past used the dark to incubate creative inspiration, underworld helpers can aid us in finding our means of expression.

Other Matrices to Explore

If you study astrology, a set of opposites that may interest you is the division of the zodiacal signs—the pairing of opposites.

TABLE 2.5—OPPOSITES OF ZODIAC SIGNS

Day houses	Night houses
Aries	Libra
Taurus	Scorpio
Gemini	Sagittarius
Cancer	Capricorn
Leo	Aquarius
Virgo	Pisces

List of Correspondences for the Number Two

Astrology: Moon, Taurus

Colors: Light blue, orange, yellow

Day of the week: Monday

Element: Water

Energy: Feminine

Gemstones: Moonstone, star ruby, turquoise

Message: "I share"

Months: February, November

Pythagorean name: Duad

Rune: Hagalaz

Tarot: High Priestess

The Three-Part Altar

The Number Three

Three is significant in Greek mythology, as we see with the three Graces, the three Gorgones, the three Furies, and the first three immortals.[1] In a Babylonian creation myth, the principal god, Marduk, "established the months and allotted three stars to each."[2] The Egyptian trinity of Ptak, Seker, and Osiris represented opening/birth, death, and resurrection.[3] In many instances, a powerful god or goddess was represented as a triad.

Buddhist canonical literature was traditionally called the *tripitaka*, or the three baskets.[4] Buddhist nun Faith Adiele says that "life in the temple is organized in threes," referring to owning three robes, bowing three times before meditation, chanting three verses, and studying the *tripitaka*.[5] The three "jewels" on the Buddhist altar are symbolic offerings that represent the body (statue of Buddha), speech (scriptural text), and the mind (a miniature stupa).[6]

For Christians, there is faith, hope, and charity, as well as the three magi who arrived at the birthplace of Jesus. A rosary meditation technique

---

1 John H. Conway and Richard K. Guy, *The Book of Numbers*, 61.

2 W. M. O'Neil, *Early Astronomy from Babylonia to Copernicus*, 18.

3 E. A. Wallis Budge, *Egyptian Magic*, 84–85.

4 Kulananda, *Principles of Buddhism*, 17.

5 Faith Adiele, *Meeting Faith*, 169.

6 Robert Beer, *The Handbook of Tibetan Buddhist Symbols*, 49.

TABLE 3.1—DIVINE TRIPLES

Names	Origin
Danu, Brigid, Mab (sometimes the Morrigan)	Celtic Ireland
Fotla, Erin, Banba	Celtic Ireland
Brahma, Vishnu, Shiva	Hindu
Al-Itab, Al-Uzza, Al-Manat	Pre-Islamic Arabian
Savaswathi, Lakshmi, Parvati	Hindu
God, Christ, Holy Spirit	Christian
Amida, Sheishi, Kwannon	Mahayana Buddhism, Japan

involves the fifteen mysteries of contemplation divided into three chaplets: the Joyful, Sorrowful, and Glorious.[7]

Pagans acknowledge a three-part cycle of life, death, and rebirth and phases of the goddess as maiden, mother, and crone. There are three levels on the Druidic path: Bard, Ovate, and Druid. Both Celtic Pagans and Irish Christians used triads for teaching and learning.

There are three primary colors: blue, red, and yellow. Three is the sum of a beginning, middle, and end. Three is the first number that produces a geometric shape: the triangle. In Neolithic cultures of the Mediterranean, this shape (the pubic triangle) represented fertility.[8] As the product of 2 + 1, three represents the triad of female, male, and offspring—creative power at its fullest extent.

Reflecting the Pythagorean belief that three means completion, a marriage was considered incomplete until there was a child. The triad also represents a new unity that does not discard the polarity of two but rather integrates it into a new whole.

---

7 Michael Glazier and Monika K. Hellwig, *The Modern Catholic Encyclopedia*, 756.

8 Marija Gimbutas, *The Language of the Goddess*, 3.

TABLE 3.2—DIVINE PROCREATIVE POWERS

Goddess	God	Offspring	Origin
Tiamat	Apsu	Mummu	Babylonian
Danu	Bíle	Lugh, Lludd, & Llevelys	Celtic/Irish
Boann	Dagda	Angus Mac Og, Brigid	Celtic/Irish
Rhiannon	Pwyll	Pryderi	Celtic/Welsh
Isis	Osiris	Horus	Egyptian
Parvati	Shiva	Ganesha	Hindu
Frigg	Odin	Balder, Thor	Norse
Olokun	Olorun	Obatala	Yoruba

In addition to the triangle, other symbols of three include the fleur-de-lis, shamrock, trefoil, and trident.[9] Simple trefoil rosette windows grace many Gothic cathedrals. The triskele that symbolized the sky above, the earth beneath, and sea around, by which many would take an oath in pre-Christian Ireland, later came to represent the Holy Trinity. The shamrock is a symbol of Ireland and of its lush green beauty—growth and manifestation. To be "in clover" is to have an easy time. The three-leaf clover or shamrock is the symbol of the Girl Scouts and Girl Guides—growth into wisdom.

At the other end of the spectrum is the notion that bad things happen in threes. With this in mind, perhaps it is no accident that the danger symbol for radiation is a rigid trefoil or shamrock-like design, and that three sixes represent the Antichrist.

The vesica piscis, the "mystical almond shape" created by two overlapping circles, represents a spiritual portal that is formed when two polarities come into balance: from two comes one. It was used in medieval Europe to symbolize "the Lord in glory."[10]

---

9 F. R. Webber, *Church Symbolism*, 44–45.
10 Ibid., 163.

Figure 3.1—The vesica piscis and the triskele.

Like the triskele, the vesica piscis may actually be an older symbol that the "new" religion adopted from the old one. The almond-shaped yoni symbol dates back to the Neolithic (and possibly beyond), to the worship of the Great Mother Goddess. A yoni, or the mystic almond, created by two circles combines the fertile creative power of the vulva with the energy of the waxing and waning moon. This symbol is incorporated into the covering of the Chalice Well in Glastonbury, England. In medieval art, the Christ child was frequently surrounded by the vesica piscis and superimposed over Mary's womb.[11] The vesica piscis represents both Christ's entry into and departure from this world.

From Hindu practices comes the three *gunas*, which can be understood as the threads out of which the cosmos is formed as well as three inherent qualities: *tamas*, or matter/groundedness; *rajas*, or energy/movement and activity; and *sattva*, or consciousness/calm awareness.[12] The ancient Ayurvedic system of health from India works with three *doshes* (vata, pitta, kapha), fundamental energies that are present in everything in varying amounts.[13]

Mathematically, the number three ("the power of three") is the agent that makes things happen. Two ones give rise to the number two

---

11 Barbara G. Walker, *The Women's Encyclopedia of Myths and Secrets*, 313–314.

12 Anodea Judith, *Wheels of Life*, 30.

13 Vasant Lad, *The Complete Book of Ayurvedic Home Remedies*, 11.

$(1 + 1 = 2)$ and one plus two gives rise to three. From there it is three that becomes the key to the higher numbers: $3 + 1 = 4$, $3 + 2 = 5$, $3 + 3 = 6$, $3 + 4 = 7$, and so on. In Jain number theory, there are three kinds of numbers: enumerable, nonenumerable, and infinite.[14]

Basic Associations

completeness	growth	triples (body/mind/
creativity	harmony	spirit, life/death/
family	manifestation	resurrection, past/
fertility	regeneration	present/future,
fulfillment		beginning/middle/
		end)

Using the Three-Part Altar

Balancing Energies

Because of the many triple aspects of gods/goddesses, powers, and mysteries in religion, myth, philosophy, and science, the three-part altar has a wide range of applications. We will begin with a simple vertical division of the altar top. As with the two-part altar, you can create areas with the placement of relevant objects or set up more visual cues by creating dividing lines with sticks, tape, or different colors of paper. Setting up the altar top does not have to be an excruciatingly difficult mathematical project. The areas should be relatively equal, but they do not have to be exact down to the last square millimeter. If it looks and feels right to you, then it is appropriate.

For many followers of Pagan paths, a three-part altar is somewhat common. However, there are diverse opinions as to which sides should be assigned to the Goddess and God. For consistency in this book, I have placed the Goddess on the right side. If your tradition, practice, or intuition tells you otherwise, then it is important for you to follow that.

---

14 John McLeish, *Number*, 118.

Although it is common for Pagans, this application can be used regardless of your spiritual path, because it also deals with balancing male and female energy. Everybody has both energies, regardless of gender. Bringing them into balance helps us accept all aspects of ourselves. When working with this setup, you can think in terms of integrating God and Goddess qualities into your life, the yogic concept of male and female energy traveling up the *ida* and *pingala* as they twine around the *sushumna* along your spine, or simply the different energies merging peacefully into your life. Because of the rushed and crazy world we live in, this type of meditation and visualization is helpful to perform from time to time for grounding and for coming back into balance. If you practice yoga, you may want to do this meditation after a session.

If you are using objects on your altar, place something that represents you in the center section. Other objects may represent your choice of deities or things that symbolize male and female energy. More simply, you could use three slips of paper: one with your name, the others with names of deities or just "woman" and "man" or "female energy" and "male energy." If you are Christian, Mary and Jesus may represent this energy. Use whatever has meaning for you.

Begin as you would for other meditations. When you are ready, focus first on whichever energy is stronger for you. Gently guide your attention to the other side of your altar and focus on that energy until it is as strong as the first. This may take a little longer; be patient. When both energies feel equal, imagine them flowing over their respective boundaries and into the center area of the altar. It may be helpful to visualize this as a gently moving white fog (think dry ice) or a soft light. Alternatively, you may imagine each of the two energies as different colors merging into white as they meet in the center. Feel this white energy flow from the middle section of your altar into your heart center.

In concert with this, you can visualize energy moving along the *ida* and *pingala* channels in your body, beginning with whichever is stronger for you. Focus on its respective side of your altar as you simultaneously feel that energy at the base of your spine. Focus on the other side and its

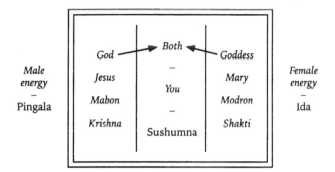

Figure 3.2—A three-part setup.

energy until it feels as strong as the first. When they seem equal, visualize them moving up their respective channels, flowing back and forth as they pass each chakra. These energies come together at the third eye chakra in the center of the forehead. As this occurs, visualize the center section of your altar filling with soft white light.

For both visualizations, when you feel the energies merge, hold it at that level for several full, deep breaths or as long as it seems appropriate for you. Slowly let it subside down through your body. Sit a while longer and enjoy the grounded feeling of wholeness.

Decision-Making Meditation

A three-part setup can be useful for deciding between two choices. However, a lot of the work for this is done before you set up your altar. Even if there are objects that you can use to symbolize each choice, begin with paper and pen.

On one sheet of paper, write down one choice and why it would be good as well as any negative aspects, and then do the same for the other choice. You don't have to create full dissertations; keywords will do. The purpose is to bring each one clearly into your mind. Set up your altar using these papers and any objects you feel are appropriate. Place a candle, preferably a taper, in the center section.

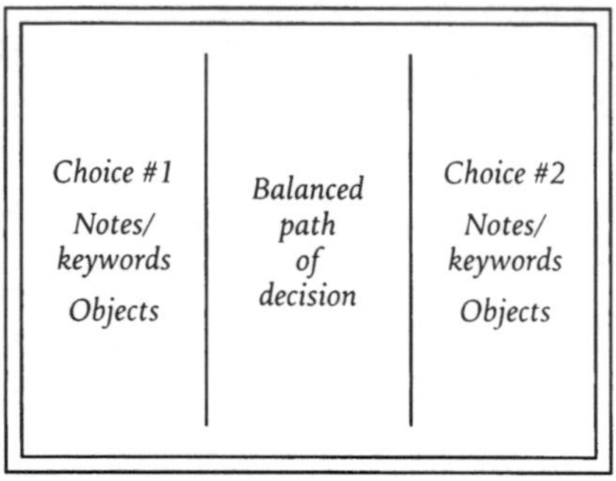

Figure 3.3—Meditation aid for decision making.

Once your altar is set up, take time to ground and center your energy and clear other thoughts from your mind. Light the candle. The purpose of writing notes or keywords for each choice was to get as much as possible fresh in your mind. Now, go through each choice in your mind as you visualize the potential outcomes. Think of the center section with the candle as a set of scales. Which choice weighs more heavily and which one feels lighter and more suitable for you? When you have reached a decision or at least feel that you are moving toward one of the choices, blow out the candle and focus on that choice. When it feels appropriate, end your meditation.

Other Vertical Setup Applications

The three-part altar is helpful for meditations that give you perspective or provide qualities on which to focus. For example, in Buddhism the three principles that are fundamental prerequisites for achieving nirvana are as follows:

- *Shila*—moral conduct, abstaining from harmful action
- *Samadhi*—mental concentration, having a disciplined mind, focusing the mind away from desires and negative action

TABLE 3.3—FURTHER MEDITATIONS

Altar section representations	Particular application
Past/present/future	A New Year's meditation
Ancestors or parents/you/children	Birthday celebration
Life/death/resurrection of Christ	Christian
Father/Son/Holy Spirit	Christian
A life of virtue, wisdom, and meditation	Buddhism—the three spiritual trainings
Mirror/sword/jewel Truth/courage/compassion	Japanese—the three treasures
Buddha, dharma, samgha (community)	Buddhism—sources of salvation
Maiden/mother/crone	Pagan—modern goddess aspects
Life giver/death wielder/transformer	Pagan—ancient goddess aspects
Youth/father/sage	Pagan—modern god aspects
Birch/oak/yew	Druidic trees
Oak/ash/thorn	Faery trees

- *Prajna*—wisdom, an honesty that allows you to see what is true and not have illusions about self[15]

Table 3.3 provides more ideas, some of which are specific to certain spiritual traditions and beliefs. As with other meditations and visualizations, placing a symbolic object in each section enhances your focus and experience.

Horizontal Setup Applications

Even though the altar top is a flat surface, with horizontal applications we need to think three-dimensional. As with the two-part altar, the three-part can be used for work with angels and faeries. This setup also makes available the three realms for shamanic journeying.

---

15 Malcolm David Eckel, *Buddhism*, 59.

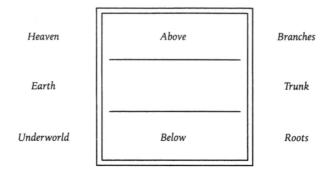

Figure 3.4—The three realms.

For shamanic work, many people use the concept of a World Tree to reach other realms of consciousness. The earthly plane of the shamanic journey exists on our everyday level, and yet it is separate. If you are used to journeying with your eyes closed, it may take some practice to do it with them open. Remember to use a "soft" gaze, with which you don't try to focus clearly on an object. Choose objects and colors (if this is important to you) for each section of the altar. Use any audio aid to which you are accustomed. Have a journal or notebook handy to record your experience.

When you settle in front of the altar, close your eyes until you begin to feel the shift in consciousness. Gently open your eyes and let your gaze move first to the center section, as it coincides with the everyday earthly plane. Let your eyes and mind take you above or below where the journey leads. When you return, record your experience. As with any journey, details will fade quickly from mind. If you usually keep a journal of your journeys, compare how this one may have been different from others.

A Christian alternative to the three realms setup is the threefold universe as envisioned by Raymond Lull, a fourteenth-century Hermeticist.[16] This is depicted in Table 3.4.

16 David Allen Hulse, *The Western Mysteries*, 123.

TABLE 3.4—LULL'S THREEFOLD UNIVERSE

Terrestrial	Celestial	Super-celestial
Humans	Angels	God
Son	Holy Spirit	Father
Body	Soul	Spirit

For those who follow a Druidic path, the three horizontal sections can be used to represent the physical world and the three permanent elements: air (sky), earth (land), and water (sea). For meditations or solo rituals held indoors, you can visualize a *nemeton*, a sacred grove of trees or clearing in the woods, with the aid of your altar. Several oak leaves and acorns in the sky sector can symbolize this sacred tree reaching up and bringing a piece of heaven to earth. A bowl of water in the water sector can represent a holy well, or add a little sea salt to honor Lir.

Alternative Matrices

The altar top does not have to be sectored into horizontal or vertical parts. This becomes especially useful when contemplating something of a cyclical nature. For example, at Samhain a Pagan may want to contemplate the eternal spiral of life, death, and rebirth. Meditating on the three aspects of the Goddess as well as any triple goddess or god would also go well with this setup. According to Frank MacEowen, there are three conditions for those on a Celtic spiritual path: "An opening within the human heart, a sheltering sense of solace in the world for those who struggle, and an ongoing sensual celebration of the beauty of life."[17] This configuration is also conducive for studying and contemplating the Celtic triads (in Pagan or Christian form). Begin in the upper center triangle and move clockwise.

---

17 Frank MacEowen, *The Mist-Filled Path*, xxiv.

Three things without which there
can be nothing good:

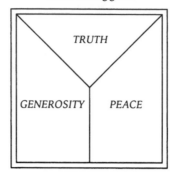

Figure 3.5—A method for contemplating the Celtic triads.

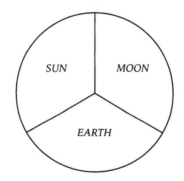

Figure 3.6—A round altar for any meditation of a cyclical nature.

This setup, of course, works very well on a round altar table, which is conducive for cyclical meditation. A special meditation on our three most significant heavenly bodies works particularly well on a round table.

You may want to experiment with different configurations, such as using the alternative layout for the purposes mentioned in the sections on vertical and horizontal setups. Allow your imagination and intuition to guide you; there is no right or wrong way to use these altar configurations.

List of Correspondences for the Number Three

Astrology: Gemini, Jupiter, Saturn, Venus

Colors: Crimson, orange, violet, yellow

Day of the week: Wednesday

Elements: Earth, fire

Energy: Masculine

Gemstones: Hematite, onyx, pearl, star sapphire, topaz

Message: "I express"

Months: December, March

Pythagorean name: Triad

Rune: Uruz

Tarot: Empress

The Four-Part Altar

The Number Four

The Pythagoreans sometimes called four "even-even" and believed it to be the number of the material world.[1] The square was the symbol for earth in a number of ancient cultures, perhaps because earthbound creatures have four legs.[2] Humans have four limbs and four chambers of the heart. The fourth chakra is the heart center.

In Western traditions, there are four elements: air, earth, fire, and water. Other "fours" of note include the seasons, the cardinal directions, times of day (dawn, midday, dusk, midnight), and moon phases (full, waning, new, waxing). The Sumerians' four seasons were marked by the risings of four constellations: spring, the bull of heaven; summer, the great lion; autumn, the scorpion; and winter, the ibex.[3] In the Hindu depiction of the Cosmic Dance, which symbolizes the destruction and re-creation of the material world,[4] Shiva is shown with four arms.

Four rivers flowing from the paradise of Eden are mentioned in the Bible: Euphrates, Gihon, Hiddekel, and Pison (Genesis 2:10 14). Virgil, Dante, and Plato wrote of the four rivers of hell: Acheron, Cocytus, Phlegethon, and Styx. Buddhist legend tells of four sacred streams flowing

---

1 John H. Conway and Richard K. Guy, *The Book of Numbers*, 63.

2 Annemarie Schimmel, *The Mystery of Numbers*, 90.

3 W. M. O'Neil, *Early Astronomy from Babylonia to Copernicus*, 17.

4 Annemarie Schimmel, *The Mystery of Numbers*, 90.

from the Damba Tree of Life. In Tibetan Buddhism, there are four transforming thoughts for daily meditation, which are known as the "four mind changers."[5]

Among the many occurrences of four in Christianity, there are four Gospels, four Evangelists, and four archangels. The four horsemen of the apocalypse rush through the four corners of the earth, destroying the material world.[6] The Bible itself can be interpreted in four ways: allegorical, historical, moral, and anagogic.[7]

Ancient Egyptians believed four great pillars held the heavens aloft, and Amon-Re was known as "the lord of the four directions."[8] According to the Maya, four giants supported the celestial realm. Taoists believed there were four guardians of the heavenly realm.[9] The Norse creation myth says that the sky is supported by four dwarfs, each of which are associated with a cardinal direction.[10]

Tetra means "four," and a tetragram is a word of four letters. "Four" itself is a tetragram. Four is the only number with a letter count equal to its value. It is the first non-prime number. It results from $2 + 2$, 2×2, and 2^2. The fourth dimension is said to be time.

Basic Associations

balance	double duality	stability
concrete reality	luck (four-leaf clover)	strength
dedication	manifestation	symmetry
dependability	order	unity

---

5 Lama Surya Das, *Awakening the Buddha Within*, 126–127.

6 Annemarie Schimmel, *The Mystery of Numbers*, 104.

7 Ibid., 94.

8 Ibid., 91.

9 Pierre Honore, *In Quest of the White God*, 35.

10 John Lindow, *Handbook of Norse Mythology*, 101.

Using the Four-Part Altar

The Four Elements and Directions

Although the basic four-part altar has two simple setups, their applications are numerous. A fairly common one is to work with each of the four Western elements to bring ourselves into balance with the natural world by creating a pattern for our minds and energy.

The altar itself can be oriented to the cardinal directions to help draw on the archetypal energy of each along with its corresponding element. Because there is a plethora of associations with the elements and directions, Table 4.1 offers a brief list, which can be easily combined with attributes from the other tables in this chapter.

A candle can be placed in each sector (according to associated colors) and lit as you focus on that element. These can be extinguished all at once at the end of your meditation or individually as you move on to each succeeding element. Objects for each element can be a representation of the entries in Table 4.1 or simply the name of the element. Alternatively, there are symbols for each element. Figure 4.2 provides a few. Use associations that resonate most deeply for you in your meditation.

You can decide ahead of time the order in which you will proceed with each element—perhaps according to a certain practice or tradition you follow—or you can allow yourself to spontaneously meditate on each element

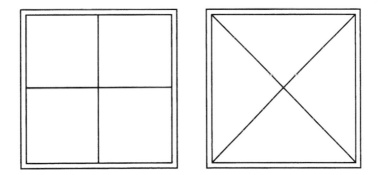

Figure 4.1—Two basic setups for the four-part altar.

TABLE 4.1—CORRESPONDENCES FOR THE ELEMENTS AND DIRECTIONS

	Physical		*Ethereal*	
	Earth	Water	Fire	Air
Direction	North	West	South	East
Season	Winter	Autumn	Summer	Spring
Attributes	Stability, foundation, nurturing	Flowing, cleansing, healing	Energetic, purification	Movement, gentleness
Colors	Green, brown, black	Blue, gray, gray-green, indigo	Red, orange, gold	Yellow, white, pastels
Goddesses	Demeter, Gaia, Ceredwen, Rhea	Aphrodite, Isis, Brigid, Danu	Brigid, Hestia, Pele, Vesta	Aradia, Arianhrod, Nuit
Gods	Arawn, Bíle, Cernunnos, Herne, Pan	Lir/Llyr, Manannan, Neptune, Poseidon	Agni, Frey, Horus, Vulcan	Enlil, Mercury, Thoth
Celestial body	Saturn	Moon, Venus	Mars, Sun	Mercury, Jupiter
Sense	Touch	Taste	Sight	Smell
Gemstones	Diamond, tourmaline	Opal, sapphire	Garnet, peridot, ruby	Agate, beryl
Animals	Bear, stag	Salmon, snake	Bull, lion	Eagle, owl
Tree	Oak	Willow		
Human	Body	Soul	Spirit	Mind

according to what you feel at the time. Alternatively, you can simply follow the order given here. Allow yourself as much time as you feel you need with each.

Once you are settled in front of your altar, close your eyes for a few minutes and clear your mind. When you feel ready, open your eyes and focus your attention on the object or objects in the earth sector of your altar. Earth represents the body—the physical. Its energy is the simplicity of everyday life. Earth is our foundation. It is the profound beauty of

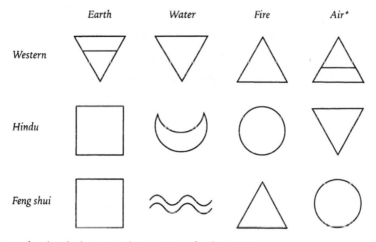

In feng shui, the element "metal" is sometimes referred to as "air."

Figure 4.2—Elemental symbols.

our existence as embodied spirit. Earth's bounty nourishes us and provides us with endless beauty. Feel the energy of earth.

Let your eyes move to the object or objects in the fire sector of your altar. Fire represents sensation and energy. It activates. It is the spark of life and the power of faith. It provides light for self-examination. It is a brilliant force that purifies and provides new beginnings. Fire nurtures us by keeping us warm, cooking our food, and giving us light. Feel the energy of fire.

Let your eyes move to the object or objects in the air sector of your altar. Air represents the mind and perception. It is inspiration and illumination. It is the storehouse of knowledge and the keeper of memories. It is communication, through which we can share the wonder and awe of our journey. Air joins us when we enter this world and is our constant companion until the end. Feel the energy of air.

Let your eyes move to the object or objects in the water sector of your altar. Water represents emotions and intuition. It is both mystery and mysterious. It gives shape to our inner worlds and meaning to our existence. It encompasses and completes us. Cleansing and comforting, water quenches our thirst and helps everything grow. Feel the energy of water.

When you have worked through all four elements, take time to remain with any thoughts or feelings that may have surfaced. If you keep a journal, record these. When you feel that your meditation is complete, ground your energy.

The Winds

Rather than associating elements with the directions, some may find it more logical to think in terms of the winds. Prior to the magnetic compass, a "wind rose" on maps helped orient the user. North was marked with a fleur-de-lis. The length and thickness of the lines radiating from the center were proportional to the wind's strength and frequency.[11]

Homer is said to have named the four principal winds, although over time and in different countries they were given various names. In classical times, the winds were believed to be immortals that chose bodies of air. They personified the power of nature and turned the wheel of time. According to E. A. Wallis Budge, in ancient Egypt "the north wind belonged to Osiris, the south wind to Ra, the west wind to Isis, and the east wind to Nephthys."[12]

In the Bible, the winds are sometimes used to represent chaos and upheaval. However, in classical myths, thirty-two different winds were used to personify gods, goddesses, and others of renown. To Native Americans, the four winds represent the energy paths of the elements. The lines that bisect the medicine wheel represent the winds. Various symbols have been used to represent winds, such as an equal-armed cross (also a symbol for fire and the sun) and the swastika.

Zoroastrians used the square to symbolize earth as four winds. Many artists used winged beasts and angels to represent them. The Hyperboreans were known as the "People Beyond the North Wind." Although of Chinese

---

11 *Encyclopedia Britannica Micropaedia*, 15th ed., s.v. "Wind Rose."
12 E. A. Wallis Budge, *Egyptian Magic*, 110.

TABLE 4.2—NAMES OF THE PRINCIPAL FOUR WINDS

	North	East	South	West
Greek	Boreas	Eurus	Notos	Zephyrus
Latin	Aquilo	Argestes	Austerus	Favonius
Italian	Tramontana	Levante	Ostro	Ponente
Celtic	Tuath	Airt	Deas	Iar

TABLE 4.3—ATTRIBUTES, ASSOCIATIONS, AND DEPICTIONS OF THE WINDS

	North	East	South	West
This wind brings	Transformation, wisdom	Change, clarity, courage	Love, harmony, fulfillment	Hope, balance to uneasy emotions
This wind aids	Intuition, faith	Personal growth, new ventures	Relationships, imagination	Confidence
Type of wind	Cold, dry	Hot, moist	Hot, dry	Cold, wet
Depiction on the Tower of Winds*	Man blowing through a sea shell	Young man ladened with fruit and grain	A water bearer emptying a vessel	Young man scattering flowers

The Tower of the Winds was built in Athens, Greece, circa 100 BCE and is still standing.

origin, "spiritually endowed" creatures represent the four directions and surround the central "wind horse" on Tibetan prayer flags. These creatures are a dragon (east), phoenix (south), tiger (west), and snow lion (north). The wind horse itself represents vital life-force energy.[13]

Set up your altar in either of the previously mentioned basic formats, using elemental objects, symbols mentioned here, or any other items that personify the winds for you. Alternatively, you can write the names on slips of paper and use in place of objects. As with the elemental meditation, take your time and focus on each section of your altar as you contemplate the

---

13 Robert Beer, *The Handbook of Tibetan Buddhist Symbols*, 67.

TABLE 4.4—CORRESPONDENCES AND ASSOCIATIONS OF THE FOUR MAJOR ARCHANGELS

	Raphael	Michael	Gabriel	Uriel
Life qualities	Faith	Hope	Charity	Understanding
Needed for happiness	Peace of mind	Courage of conviction	Love within the heart	Strength of resolve
Truths from the angels	Peace through faith	Courage through hope	Love through charity	Strength through resolve
Known as	The Healer	The Warrior-Protector	The Messenger	The Light of God
His symbols	Staff, flask, fish	Dragon, scales, sword	Lily, shield, trumpet	Flame, sword
Earthly elements	Air	Fire	Water	Earth

TABLE 4.5—THE FOUR NOBLE TRUTHS

Life is difficult and full of suffering.	Because we are embodied spirit, there are many things that happen to us on the emotional, psychological, and physical levels that may be difficult. It is important to balance these with the good things that occur.
Suffering comes from attachment.	A lot of our suffering comes from the belief that we have to have certain things or people in our lives, or that we have to be a certain way.
Suffering can be ended.	Learning to distinguish need from desire is a vital lesson that can put us on the path to freedom.
There is a path to end suffering.	Accepting ourselves and striving to be a good person helps us along the path to freedom. In addition, finding the middle of the path is important so we do not get swept away by either excess of greedy self-indulgence or ascetic self-mortification. The path includes compassion, virtue, wisdom, and meditation.

attributes or other associations you already hold for each wind. At the end, take time to assess your energy.

Archangels

To Christians, angels are generally believed to be messengers from God, and there are many types of angels. The archangels have always been considered leaders and thought to be very powerful. They are said to control the energy of the elements. Many people seek to work with angelic energy for healing, peace, and protection, as well as for spiritual reasons.

Angels can be invoked by repeating their names, and they frequently come unbidden when needed. Angelic energy can help us find certain qualities within ourselves.

The Four Noble Truths

According to Lama Surya Das, the Four Noble Truths are the core of Buddha's teaching, and they contain all that is necessary for enlightenment.[14] Central to this is the belief that unhappiness can be overcome through spiritual means and that much of our unhappiness and difficulties come from our desires. This is an especially important lesson when it comes to material desires. Our culture is a perpetual wheel of *samsara*, the doctrine of rebirth, "an eternal grind of deaths and potential suffering."[15] It is so easy to be caught up in this and to continuously chase after things that we don't have but believe we need.

The Four-Fold Way

The Four-Fold Way was created by cultural anthropologist Angeles Arrien, PhD, as a way to reclaim our mythological roots in order to access the four archetypal patterns that support physically, emotionally, spiritually, and mentally healthy lives. The four archetypes of warrior, healer, visionary, and

---

14 Lama Surya Das, *Awakening the Buddha Within*, 75–94.

15 Malcolm David Eckel, *Buddhism*, 89.

TABLE 4.6—ASPECTS AND ASSOCIATIONS OF THE FOUR-FOLD WAY

Archetype	Aspects	Ways to live	Basic principles	The elements	The directions
Warrior	Power, service	Right action	Show up	Air	North
Healer	Acknowledgment, love	Right speech	Pay attention	Earth	South
Visionary	Truthfulness, integrity	Right placement	Tell the truth	Fire	East
Teacher	Wisdom, guidance	Right timing	Open to outcome	Water	West

TABLE 4.7—THE FOUR AGREEMENTS

"Be impeccable with your word."	Our word is our power and integrity. What we say expresses our intent about ourselves and others. Intent is the first step to manifesting an idea or belief into our world. Speech can be an instrument of fear for others, it can be self-deprecating, or it can be a tool for truth and love.
"Don't take anything personally."	It is a rough-and-tumble world out there, and we can be bruised by the careless words and intent of others. Learning to stand strong, supported by our core of self-love and integrity, saves us from so much needless suffering.
"Don't make assumptions."	This one is all about communication, especially the ability to voice our needs and desires in a clear, honest way. Being clear with others avoids many misunderstandings that can cloud our day-to-day journey.
"Always do your best."	No one can honestly expect more from us, and neither can we. Although doing our best can vary from time to time, knowing that we took responsibility for our actions and made a good effort allows us to live in truth and with integrity.

teacher are parts of a whole to which we can aspire. Balancing these parts can be achieved by living the four basic principles:

- Show up and choose to be present.
- Pay attention to things that have heart and true meaning.
- Be truthful and without blame or judgment.
- Be open to the outcome of any situation rather than being attached to a specific result.[16]

The Four Agreements

In his book *The Four Agreements*, Don Miguel Ruiz provides inspiration for daily life through wisdom from the Toltec people of Mexico. Although the agreements may seem a simple creed by which to live, each one requires deep thought and true commitment. Mr. Ruiz states that "all of humanity is searching for truth, justice and beauty: but we fail to see that everything is already within us."[17] The four agreements provide a path to truth, justice, and beauty as well as a means to bring these qualities out to the surface to guide us. Allow yourself time to contemplate these qualities and how you may currently measure up to them, and then, if it is appropriate, make the agreements with your soul.

Allowing Self to Rise

Quite frequently, the inability to move forward in life is not due to someone else holding us back: all too often, we do a fine job of this on our own. Many times, it is a matter of being afraid to let go. This could be letting go of the past, inaccurate self-images, people, situations, or emotions. At some point, we need to come to terms with whatever it is we are holding on to. It may be necessary to spend time in meditation to clarify the

---

16 Angeles Arrien, *The Four-Fold Way*.

17 Don Miguel Ruiz, *The Four Agreements*, 15.

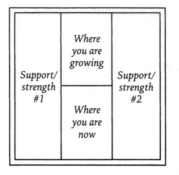

Figure 4.3—A four-part altar for moving forward and growing.

issue or situation for ourselves first. The following are important points to identify:

- Who am I now; what is holding me back; what is my current situation/status

- What person could I be (better yet, who am I, truly); how will I evolve/grow; what will be changed in my life

- What are two sources of support such as a sibling and a friend, spouse/partner and child, spirituality and work; think in terms of where your strength comes from—it may even be yourself

Set up your altar with objects, colors, symbols, or written statements and keywords for each sector. Prepare for meditation or visualization. Contemplate where you are now. Bring it clearly into your mind. When you feel that it is well defined, move your gaze and thoughts to one of your sources of support or strength. Visualize how it helps you and how it will aid in your letting go of whatever prevents you from moving forward. When it is clear in your mind, repeat with the second source of support or strength. When that is also clear to you, move your gaze and thoughts to the final sector of the altar. Feel yourself becoming and accepting your true self, a changed situation, or a new path. Feel deep

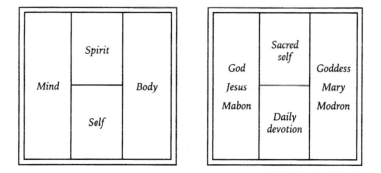

Figure 4.4—The four-part altar for integration of
self and integration of sacred with everyday self.

within your soul what it is that you are moving toward. Know that you
can get there.

When you feel that you "know" this, close your eyes and take that feeling to heart. Know deep within yourself that you hold the keys to your
own growth and transformation. Sit with this thought for a few minutes
as you breathe deeply and slowly. Bring your attention back to the room,
and then open your eyes and give yourself a hug.

In our rushed world, it is easy to feel fractured and out of touch with
ourselves. Because of this, it is helpful to virtually pull ourselves together,
metaphorically and/or spiritually. The example altars in Figure 4.4 can
be assigned and worked with in any fashion or order that appeals to you.
Spend equal time with each sector and then contemplate the whole. If
these are meditations that you repeat from time to time, you may want to
journal your experience afterward.

Medicine Wheel and Solar Disk

A circle divided into four is an important symbol for followers of Native
American and Celtic paths.

The medicine wheel symbol comes from the Plains Indians and was
commonly used in ceremonial artwork. It was a symbol of power worn
by warriors and painted on their shields. Ancient stone medicine wheels

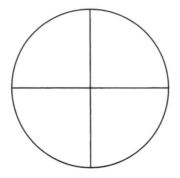

Figure 4.5—Native American medicine wheel or Celtic solar disk.

TABLE 4.8—SECTORS OF THE NATIVE AMERICAN MEDICINE WHEEL

East	South	West	North
Red	Yellow	White	Black
Child	Adolescent	Adult	Elder
Physical	Social	Intellectual	Spiritual
Sacrifice	Prayer	Transformation	Thanksgiving
Receives energy	Determines energy	Gives energy	Holds energy
Sunrise, new beginnings, birth	Warmth, creativity, nurturing	Sunset, freedom, spaciousness	Moonlight, wisdom, openness

have been found from Canada to New Mexico and along the Mississippi floodplain. The most famous is in the Big Horn Mountains of Wyoming. Some of these wheels have astronomical significance.[18]

The Crow Indians' name for the medicine wheel meant "Sun's Tipi," and in addition to marking the sunrise on the summer solstice, the medicine wheels also marked the risings of three stars: Aldebaran in Taurus, Rigel in Orion, and Sirius in Canis Major.[19] The wheels were used for tribal gatherings, vision quests, and healing.

---

18 E. Barrie Kavasch, *The Medicine Wheel Garden*, 7.

19 Ibid., 9.

TABLE 4.9—CELTIC ASSOCIATIONS FOR THE FOUR-PART ROUND ALTAR

Direction	Quarter day	Animal	Mystical city	Treasure	Archetype
East	Spring equinox (Alban Eilir)	Crow	Gorias	Sword of Nuadu	Healer
South	Summer solstice (Alban Hefin)	Stag	Finias	Spear of Lugh	Warrior
West	Autumn equinox (Alban Elfed)	Salmon	Murias	Cauldron of the Dagda	Provider
North	Winter solstice (Alban Arthan)	Bear	Falias	Lia Fail, the Stone of Destiny	Sovereignty

Containing the important lessons in life, the medicine wheel encompasses spiritual, emotional, mental, and physical components, and its study promotes personal accountability and healthy living. As there are many variations, Table 4.8 is provided as a sample. The series of four do not necessarily correspond with directions and colors. In keeping with traditional medicine wheels, you might consider using stones to mark your altar boundaries. An offering, symbol, or something from nature can be placed in each sector. Consider doing a meditation based on giving thanks for sectors that represent what you have already passed through, gratitude for your present stage in life, and hopes for those yet to come.

As a Celtic sun disk, the divided wheel represents the four solar observances or festivals. These are known as the quarter days. Like the Native American medicine wheel, the solar disk can represent the turning of the seasons as well as the cycle of life, death, transformation, and rebirth. The four-part altar with Celtic application can also represent the mystical realms and the great treasures of the Tuatha Dé Danann, a pantheon of Irish gods known as the Tribe of Danu, which can be associated with archetypal energy.

The four archetypes are discussed below.

The Healer: Being a healer is concerned with self-healing and finding the ability within. When we find this in ourselves, we can become a healing presence for others. We don't actually become healers, but instead facilitate the process in others. The healer is about the deep inner self.

The Warrior: A warrior in this sense is one who protects those who are unable to stand up for themselves—the young, elderly, and ill. The warrior is about compassion, community, and responsibility.

The Provider: To be a provider is to take care of oneself and others. More importantly, the provider is about nurturing on many levels, which is an important lesson especially for men.

Sovereignty: This is about service and commitment to honor and care for the land, but it goes beyond the concept of monarchy or nation. Sovereignty is about the living spirit of the natural world, which is our connection to the Divine.

List of Correspondences for the Number Four

Astrology: Cancer, Earth, Saturn
Colors: Green, orange, violet
Day of the week: Thursday
Element: Earth
Energy: Feminine
Gemstones: Amethyst, emerald, sapphire
Message: "I build"
Month: April
Pythagorean name: Tetrad
Rune: Dagaz
Tarot: Emperor

The Five-Part Altar

The Number Five

Five is a very personal number: we have five fingers or toes on each limb, and five senses. The pentagram, pentacle, and pentangle are various names for the five-pointed star,[1] which is sometimes depicted as the human body: the four limbs and the head. Greek philosophers described five parts of a human: physical body, animal soul, intelligence, psyche, and divine spirit. They called the pentagram a *Pentalpha* because it could be drawn with five letter As.

In the Ayurvedic system, all matter is said to be composed of five elements: air, fire, water, earth, and space.[2] In feng shui, five is the number that symbolizes center, as well as the number of basic elements: earth, fire, metal, water, and wood. Traditional Chinese medicine associates five colors with the elements as well as the five "solid" organs: heart, liver, spleen, lungs, and kidneys.[3] In ancient China, the five sacred mountains surrounding the plain of the Middle Kingdom completed the model of the physical universe.[4]

For Christians, five is symbolic of the number of wounds inflicted on Jesus upon the cross. There are five women named Mary in the New

---

1 John H. Conway and Richard K. Guy, *The Book of Numbers*, 41.

2 Vasant Lad, *The Complete Book of Ayurvedic Home Remedies*, 8.

3 Sandy Fritz, *Mosby's Fundamentals of Therapeutic Massage*, 483.

4 Edward Schafer, *Ancient China*, 102–103.

Testament. According to Buddhism, there are five great evils: anger, desire, envy, ignorance, and malevolence. The five pillars of Islam are giving alms, faith, the fast of Ramadan, the pilgrimage to Mecca, and daily ritual prayer. Prayers are made five times a day. The five books of Moses, the *Pentateuch*, are the foundation of Hebrew law and history. Collections of Hindu fables called *Pañcatantra* contain five teachings.[5] The ancient Celtic Ogham alphabet contains twenty-five characters separated into five groups of five characters.[6]

The Aztecs believed that there were five ages of the sun,[7] and a Navajo creation myth is based on five worlds.[8] The ancient Indo-Europeans marked five seasons, each with seventy-three days and noted by the meteorological information of warm, hot, rains, frosts, and mists.[9] There are five great oceans: Antarctic, Arctic, Atlantic, Indian, and Pacific. The five-ringed Olympic symbol represents the five major continents: Africa, the Americas, Asia, Australia, and Europe.

In the ancient Hindu book called the *Devi Gita* ("Song of the Goddess"), the goddess describes five basic seated yoga postures conducive for meditation and general well-being: Lotus, Hero, Diamond, Happiness, and Auspicious.[10]

Five is the fulcrum of single-digit numbers (excluding zero). As such, it is considered a point of change. When multiplied by any power of itself, it produces a number ending with five: $5 \times 5 = 25$; $5 \times 5 \times 5 = 125$. Five's geometric shape is a pentagon and is considered to be the purest form of proportion. Five also expresses the union of female (two) and male (three) energies, and to the Pythagoreans it represented marriage.[11]

5 Annemarie Schimmel, *The Mystery of Numbers*, 107–119.

6 Caitlin and John Matthews, *The Encyclopedia of Celtic Wisdom*, 50.

7 John M. Wickersham, *Myths and Legends of the World*, vol. 1, 82.

8 John H. Conway and Richard K. Guy, *The Book of Numbers*, 64.

9 W. M. O'Neil, *Early Astronomy from Babylonia to Copernicus*, 11.

10 C. MacKenzie Brown, *The Devi Gita*, 167–168.

11 John H. Conway and Richard K. Guy, *The Book of Numbers*, 64.

Basic Associations

balance	freedom	seeking
change	knowledge	speech
curiosity	logic	travel
divine grace	restlessness	

Using the Five-Part Altar

The Senses

We begin with a five-part meditation that will be common to all regardless of ethnic origin, nationality, religion, or anything else that serves to distinguish or divide us. The senses operate in two ways: they connect us with the outer world, and they help us move deeper into our inner world.

Although the senses have been blamed for being a distraction to meditation as well as a source of trouble to those trying to live an ascetic life, they are our gateway for experiencing and connecting with the world around us. As we open our senses to receive more of the world, perception of our surroundings may shift. This fuller view can hold more beauty and allow us to increase our interactions with the world. That said, it is important to learn control of this opening of the senses, because it is possible to have too much of a good thing. Learning how or when to shut down or shield ourselves is essential to avoid overstimulation and prevent overload. This is a personal process of learning, as we each have our own individual levels of tolerance.

The Sanskrit word *panchakamaguna* means "offerings of the five senses," which were said to be a collection of the most beautiful objects that captivate the senses.[12] These objects are used on Buddhist and Hindu altars as offerings to deities. In addition, the five Buddhas are each associated with one of the senses. They are included in Table 5.1.

---

12 Robert Beer, *The Handbook of Tibetan Buddhist Symbols*, 27.

Figure 5.1—The altar of the senses.

TABLE 5.1—ALTAR OBJECTS FOR THE SENSES

Sense	Items for Each Sector	How to Use
Sight	Pictures or objects	Focus upon with a soft gaze
Sound	Chimes, bell	Close eyes and listen
Smell	Flower, incense, perfume	Close eyes and experience
Taste	Juice, slice of fruit	Close eyes and experience
Touch	Stone, crystal	Close eyes and experience

Opening our senses in a calm, peaceful setting helps us move inward to discover the spark of divinity that resides at our core. Choose items (one for each sense) for your altar that will gently stimulate and open each sense. Table 5.1 offers a few suggestions, but ultimately use whatever works best and holds meaning for you.

Begin with the sight sector of the altar, which should be the farthest away from where you are seated, and work toward you. Take time to experience each object. Become aware of your energy at each level and how each sense level vibrates within you. Let each sense move you deeper into yourself as you work with it, until you feel that you have reached your soul level. Ask yourself who you are—not on the surface, but inside. Who are you to you? You may not be able to describe this verbally. It will most

TABLE 5.2—CORRESPONDENCES FOR THE SENSES

Sense	Chakra	Element (Western)	Element (Chinese)	Primal energy	Attribute	Buddha	Beautiful object
Sight	Solar plexus	Fire	Wood	Yin	Consciousness	Vairocana	Mirror
Sound	Throat	Spirit	Water	Yang	Feeling	Ratnasambhava	Lute, gong, finger symbol
Smell	Root	Air	Metal	Yang	Perception	Amitabha	Incense
Taste	Sacral	Water	Fire	Yang	Will	Amoghasiddhi	Fruit
Touch	Heart	Earth	Earth	Yin	Form	Akshobya	Silk

TABLE 5.3—ADDITIONAL FIVE-PART MEDITATIONS

Christian: The Glorious Mysteries	The Resurrection, The Ascension, Assumption of the Holy Virgin, Descent of the Holy Spirit, Crowning of Mary
	Virtue of faith, Virtue of hope, Devotion to Mary, Love of God, Eternal happiness
Tenets of Tae kwon do	Courtesy, integrity, perseverance, self-control, indomitable spirit
Buddhist	Accomplishment, discernment, equanimity, ultimate reality, mirror-like
	Mandalas of the five Buddhas: Vairochana, Amitabha, Amoghasiddhi, Akshobhya, Ratnasambhava
Confucian Virtues	Duty, wisdom, reliability, ceremony, humanity

likely be a certain feeling that you can sense from within. It may take a little time to come to you, but it will, and as it does, you will begin to sense this as your inner flame or inner light. Once you reach that inner light, draw it up through each sense level.

Enjoy this deep sense of self. Learn to cultivate and reach this level in everyday life. As you do this, you may find that you also cultivate your intuitive and psychic abilities.

The five-part altar matrix, either vertical or horizontal, can be used to meditate on sets of five in a wide variety of beliefs and disciplines. Table 5.3 provides a few suggestions.

The Fifth Part in the Center

The point at which the four cardinal directions come together has been considered the meeting point of heaven and earth in a number of cultures.[13] To the Celts of Gaul, this occurred as a natural clearing in the woods. Called *nemetons*, these places were considered extremely sacred.

The center is where we can symbolically touch the Divine. It is the power of consciousness and spirit. To the Pythagoreans, the world was

---

13 Annemarie Schimmel, *The Mystery of Numbers*, 112–113.

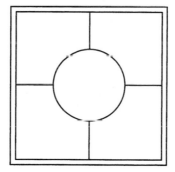

Figure 5.2—The fifth part at the center.

made up of five essences: air, fire, water, earth, and ether (*quinta essentia*), which was all-embracing and considered to be the "real element of life."[14] The word *quintessential* (concentrated essence) comes from this concept.

To section off the areas of your altar, the middle can be round or square and is easily created with a piece of paper, a dinner plate, or another flat object. This matrix can be used to meditate on the four Western elements plus spirit or self. The center also symbolizes love and compassion.

The four outer sectors of this altar matrix can be used as stepping stones or stages for entering into spirit or coming into self. These outer sectors can be perceived as the cardinal directions, elements, gifts of the Tuatha Dé Danann, or any related aspects. (See "The Four-Part Altar" for more suggestions.) Alternatively, you may want to devise your own pathway to spirit allowing each outer sector to be a gateway into the other.

Celtic Meditations

For those who are Irish, of Irish descent, or on a Celtic spiritual path, using an altar matrix that is reminiscent of Brigid's (or Saint Brigit's) cross adds a cultural dimension to your meditations. Brigid was venerated as a Celtic goddess as well as a sixth-century abbess at Kildare Ireland.[15]

---

14 Ibid., 117–118.

15 Jean Markale, *The Celts*, 145.

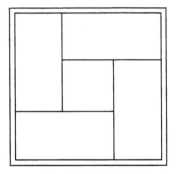

Figure 5.3—Brigid's or Saint Brigit's cross matrix.

Her cross is traditionally made from four plaited rushes extending from a square center. The elements and/or directions can be worked with in the same manner outlined above. The spirit or Divine represented in the center would, of course, be Brigid, or Saint Brigit. This can be used to honor her on Saint Brigit's Day/Imbolg (February 1st/2nd). Since she presides over crossroads, healing, and sacred waters, call on her energy if you seek guidance or at any time you need help in determining choice.

This altar matrix can also be used for the meditation of the five senses, with the center being the deepest level of touch. In Celtic mythology, it was from the Well of Segais (also known as Connla's Well) that five major streams flowed, bringing forth knowledge.

This setup can also be used for meditation on the Celtic past or your Irish heritage, with each sector representing the five ancient provinces of Ireland: Ulster, Connacht, Munster, Leinster, and Meath. The Irish word for provinces, *cóiced*, means "fifths."[16] Instead of representing the provinces, the sectors could represent five symbols of Ireland: triskele, harp, shamrock, Celtic cross, and Claddagh. You may find other "fives" related to Ireland and the Celts.

---

16 James MacKillop, *Dictionary of the Celtic Myth*, 94.

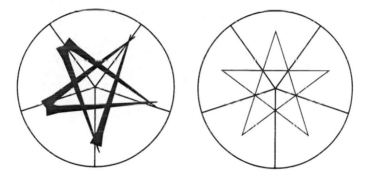

Figure 5.4—The round five-part altar can be used to celebrate the Passion of Christ or five stages of life.

In the Round

When the focus of a meditation uses an odd-numbered matrix, the round altar can be easier to set up. Circular meditations where we want to move through things more than once can flow more easily, too, since our minds don't have to kick into any linear logic (that is, "go back to the beginning"). For example, the pentagram (elements plus spirit) works very well on a round altar. Starhawk suggests a pentacle meditation on the five stages of life: birth, coming into being; initiation, adolescence, individuation; love, union, full adulthood; repose, age, reflection, wisdom; death, letting go and moving on.[17]

Until medieval times, Christians used a pentagram created with five nails to contemplate the five wounds on Jesus at his crucifixion (the five sorrowful mysteries) as well as Christ's epiphanies.[18]

Robert Graves's Celtic tree calendar includes five seasonal trees: one for each of the four seasons, plus the winter solstice, when the sun appears to stand still in the sky.[19] The altar as a wheel can also represent the five major Jewish festivals: Passover, Sukkot, Pentecost, Rosh Hashana, and Yom Kippur.

---

17 Starhawk, *The Spiral Dance*, 79.

18 Annemarie Schimmel, *The Mystery of Numbers*, 118.

19 Robert Graves, *The White Goddess*, 245–253.

TABLE 5.4—GODDESSES AND GODS PLANT ASSOCIATIONS

Plant	Goddess/God
Fig	Aphrodite, Demeter, Hathor, Juno
Ivy	Arianrhod, Bachus, Cernunnos, Danu, Rhea
Lily	Artemis, Hera, the Virgin Mary
Planetree/ sycamore	Cerridwen, Hecate, Morrigan
Rose	Venus, the Virgin Mary
Vine/bramble	Bacchus, Brigid, Freya, Llyr

TABLE 5.5—THE FIVE PRINCIPLES OF REIKI

Just for today I will . . .
. . . live in the attitude of gratitude. This encompasses being thankful for our blessings and what we have, as well as believing that the universe will provide for us.
. . . not worry. Worrying is a black hole for energy. The more energy we expend with worry, the less energy we have for living our purpose. We cannot change the past, and we can only do our best in the future.
. . . not anger. Like worry, this is a black hole for energy that can be very destructive. When this emotion arises, it is important to note it, tone it down, and deal with the issue in a constructive way rather than lashing out. It's not an easy skill to develop, but anger can be transformed. Once you are able to do it, it adds to the attitude of gratitude.
. . . do my work honestly. This has to do with facing the truth with ourselves. We must learn to see life's lessons through truthful eyes rather than fooling ourselves and living in denial. Being truthful with oneself creates loving harmony that radiates out into all aspects of life.
. . . show love and respect for all living things. All living things on this earth have worth and deserve dignity. Be aware of how you live and how it may have an impact on other people, resources, and the earth itself. We are part of the whole. To hurt others and the natural world is to hurt ourselves.

Five in Nature

The round altar also works well when using objects from the natural world as your focus of contemplation; however, any altar shape can be used. Plants with fivefold symmetry have been associated with various goddesses and gods and were believed to be especially magical. Not only does the apple flower have five petals, but the fruit, when cut in half horizontally, reveals a five-pointed star of seeds.

Like the apple, the wild rose is a member of a large group of plants called *Rosaceae*.[20] These all have five-petalled flowers and include blackberries, cherries, pears, plums, raspberries, and strawberries. While the modern cultivated rose has numerous petals, underneath them around the base of the flower you will find five sepals (modified leaves).

The rose is perhaps most widely associated with the Virgin Mary as a symbol of innocence, purity, perfection, mercy, and majesty. A natural rose has five petals or many more; however, the six-petalled rose has been a mystical symbol for centuries. (See "The Six-Part Altar.") If you are a Christian, you may find these qualities important to reflect and meditate upon. The rose and the pentacle were symbols of the sacred feminine, the goddesses Venus and Ishtar, and womanhood in general. In association with Venus, it represented beauty, physical love, and perfection.

The five-pointed star is used as a symbol by many groups: the Order of the Eastern Star, Pagans, and the Freemasons, in their flaming star. Nature also likes the five-pointed star. As previously mentioned, you will find it in a horizontally sliced apple, starfish, sand dollar, and sea urchin (underneath).

The Five Principles of Reiki

In the mid 1800s, Dr. Mikao Usui brought the practice of healing with universal life-force energy out of obscurity and named it Reiki. While developing methods for its application and observing human nature, Dr.

---

20 Thomas H. Everett, *The New York Botanical Gardens Illustrated Encyclopedia of Horticulture*, vol. 9, 2979.

Usui began to incorporate these principles into his teachings. He believed that when a person was in his or her proper flow of energy, these principles would "emanate naturally."[21] On the other hand, focusing on and living the principles would help a person get into their proper flow.

Use whichever five-part physical setup appeals to you for this meditation. Each Reiki principle written on a card and placed in the sectors of the altar can serve as reminders for you.

List of Correspondences for the Number Five

Astrology: Leo, Mars, Mercury, Venus, Taurus

Colors: Dark blue, orange

Day of the week: Tuesday

Elements: Air, fire

Energy: Masculine

Gemstones: Garnet, ruby, sardonyx, turquoise

Message: "I change"

Month: May

Pythagorean name: Pentad

Rune: Rad

Tarot: Hierophant

---

21 Paula Horan, *Empowerment through Reiki*, 44.

The
Six-Part Altar

The Number Six

For Christians, the mythical six-petalled rose represents perfection and is the emblem of the Virgin Mary and Saint Joseph. Catholics observe six holy days of obligation.[1] Zoroastrians believed in six eras of creation, with six associated angelic beings.[2]

According to Euclid, six is the first perfect number, because the numbers that divide into it add up to the number itself (1, 2, and 3). Saint Augustine believed it was perfect because God created the world in six days. Cornelius Agrippa considered it to be the number of man because God created humans on the sixth day.[3]

In the chakra system of India, the second (sacral) chakra is depicted with a six-petalled lotus. In geometry, the hexagon is formed by six equilateral triangles. A three-dimensional arrangement of these creates the star tetrahedron.[4] The hexagonal crystal structure has six faces or symmetrical exterior surfaces around its center. Quartz, aquamarine, beryl, diamond, and emerald are examples of this crystal type and are exceptionally good for use on a six-part altar.

---

1 Rev. John Trigilio Jr., PhD, and Rev. Kenneth Brighenti, PhD, *Catholicism for Dummies*, 154.

2 Annemarie Schimmel, *The Mystery of Numbers*, 124.

3 John H. Conway and Richard K. Guy, *The Book of Numbers*, 66–67.

4 Catherine Bowman, *Crystal Awareness*, 8–11.

In traditional Chinese medicine, *liu qu* are the six excesses, which are also known as the six pernicious influences. These describe environmental conditions that were considered "pathogenic factors" and consisted of wind, cold, summer heat, dampness, dryness, and fire.[5]

Six is the foundation of many designs created in nature and by humans. As previously mentioned, it is the basis of some crystals, as well as the pattern of snowflakes and honeycombs, chicken wire and nuts and bolts. It is a design of strength and efficiency. Another note: all true insects have six legs.

Basic Associations

balance	fidelity	luck
beauty	harmony	perfection
communion	healing	symmetry
devotion	longevity	sympathy
equilibrium	love	wholeness

Using the Six-Part Altar

The Planes of Movement

We frequently remain oblivious to our bodies unless something hurts. For the most part, we take for granted the heroic work of our hearts and lungs and the incredible strength of the feet and legs that carry us where we want to go. After all, we are body, mind, and spirit, and while we generally think of meditation as concerning mind and spirit, there is no reason why it cannot incorporate the body, as it is very much a part of who we are.

Our world is three-dimensional, and each plane of movement has two directions: left-right, front-back, and up-down (or upper and lower). On a personal physical level, these are also the planes in which our bodies move: coronal plane, median plane, and transverse. Contemplating these

---

5 Sandy Fritz, *Mosby's Fundamentals of Therapeutic Massage*, 484.

TABLE 6.1—THE PLANES AND MOVEMENT OF THE BODY

Plane	Divide	Location	Movement one	Example of movement one	Movement two	Example of movement two
Median/ midsagittal	Left-right	Vertical middle	Forward	Stepping forward	Backward	Hands behind back
Coronal	Front-back	Vertical perpendicular to median	Toward middle	Cross one leg over the other	Away from median	Arm raised to the side
Transverse	Upper-lower	Horizontal at waist*	Outward	Pointing foot to the side rotates leg	Inward	Shoulders forward and down

Transverse planes run throughout the body.

Left	Right
Front	Back
Upper	Lower

Figure 6.1—The physical planes matrix.

movements can be used to bring yourself fully into your body as well as honor the beautiful complexities of it.

As we age, we have a tendency to become less physically active. As a result, we lose touch with the everyday experiences with our bodies that we had as children. Sports activities are good for keeping in shape, but they are goal-oriented and not intended for focusing on the body. Eastern disciplines such as yoga, tai chi, and a plethora of martial arts are the opposite, in that it is essential to move attention inward and focus on the body. Walking and jogging can also provide opportunities to do this.

The simplest way to set up the altar for this meditation is to print the words on slips of paper and lay them out as illustrated in Figure 6.1. Alternatively, things such as rings or other jewelry worn on specific sides of your body can be used for the left and right sectors. A pendant, religious symbol, or other item that you wear on a chain can be used for the front sector while the chain itself can be used for the back. You could use a rolled-up belt or scarf for either. For the upper and lower sectors, you can use a comb, barrette, or ponytail tie and shoelaces or socks, respectively. Pictures of these objects can be cut from magazines and used as well.

Set up your altar and prepare as you normally do for meditation. When you are ready, begin to focus on left and right. You may want to think of how your body moves from side to side. Bring the sensation of that movement into your awareness. When you visualize this movement, keep it gentle. This is not an exercise video running in your head. It is coming into awareness of the subtle way in which your body moves.

If you have any physical issues or limitations, accept them with your heart. These are a part of who you are, and they are to be loved as much as the rest of you. "Limitations" can be viewed as special challenges that some of us have been given to learn specific information in this lifetime.

After you focus on a plane of movement, go a step deeper and, in turn, concentrate on each of its two parts. When you have taken it to the fullest extent, move on to the next plane. When you have worked through all three, pull back the camera of your mind's eye and contemplate all of them together. Think of the amazing range of motion available to us.

Meditating on our bodies is by its nature very grounding. However, even though the body and mind have been viewed as separate in Western culture, they are integrated parts of a whole. As a result, feelings and emotions can surface when working with the body. Emotional blocks are held within our physical selves and may be released when we work with our bodies. This is fairly common in yoga.

If this occurs while meditating, accept it, note it, and let it go. Don't try to figure out what happened or why. It just is. If nothing like this occurs, don't worry. The intent of the meditation is to move inward and appreciate ourselves. End this meditation by giving yourself a hug.

The Rosa Mystica

While the wild rose has five petals, the mythical rose of six petals came to be a metaphor for perfection and balance. The concept of a six-petalled rose could have come about from the Hebrew word *shoshana*, which means "lily" or "rose." (Although the lily appears to have six petals, it actually has three petals and three sepals that look like petals.) *Shoshan* means "lily" and *shoshahanah* means "rose."[6] The lily is also associated with the Virgin Mary as a symbol of simplicity and purity.[7]

---

6 Hayim Baltsan, *Webster's New World Hebrew Dictionary*, 404.

7 Katherine Kear, *Flower Wisdom*, 77.

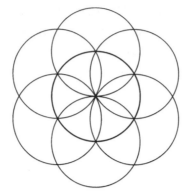

Figure 6.2—Six petals formed by circles.

Since ancient times, the rose has represented mystery and has been associated with the goddesses Aphrodite, Astarte, Ishtar, and Isis.[8] As a Marian symbol since the Middle Ages, the mystical rose became a symbol of divine love. Early Christians embraced the symbolism, distinguishing the red rose as representing the blood of Christ and the white rose the purity of Mary.[9] It was also a symbol of medieval alchemists. A six-petalled rose pattern appears in the architecture of churches. It is created by the intersection of six circles, with a seventh circle framing the petals.

In the medieval Christian labyrinth, the circuitous path leads to a six-petalled rose at the center.[10] It was sometimes called the Rose of Sharon, which was also a name given to Mary. In addition, the Rose of Sharon was also a mystical symbol for God's Holy Spirit. In the labyrinth, this rose represents the inner self—the center of the universe. Like the lotus in Eastern disciplines, the rose was associated with enlightenment. As you move toward the center of a labyrinth, you move toward self-illumination.

For the mystical rose altar setup, six crystals with the hexagonal crystal structure can greatly enhance your experience. Rose quartz is the pre-

---

8 Ibid., 211.

9 Anthony F. Chiffolo, *100 Names of Mary*, 61–62.

10 Dr. Lauren Artress, *Walking a Sacred Path*, 58.

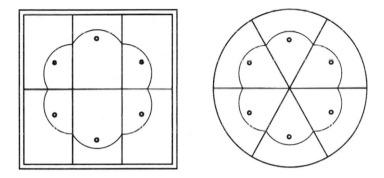

Figure 6.3—The mystical rose matrix.

TABLE 6.2—SUBJECTS FOR THE MYSTICAL ROSE MEDITATION

The Virgin Mary	Innocence, love, purity, perfection, mercy, and majesty
Six days of creation	Light; the heavens; earth and plants; sun, moon, and stars; fish and fowl; and animals and humans
Second chakra	Desires, emotions, passions, sensuality, sexuality, and (pro)creativity
Buddhist virtues to gain perfection	Charity, contemplation, energy, patience, purity, and wisdom

ferred gemstone. It has the hexagonal structure, its name is quite appropriate, and its color is soft and appealing. Along with the crystals, you may want to place a slip of paper or a folded index card with a keyword (see Table 6.2) to serve as a memory aid. This meditation can also be done with other types of crystals or with no crystals. Follow your intuition and use what feels appropriate for you.

The grid pattern on the altar does not need to be present during the meditation, but it is useful for positioning the objects. As in the previous meditation, this one is for focusing your energy inward, and its purpose is personal.

Whatever focus you choose for your six-part mystical rose meditation, let each crystal/petal/sector represent an aspect of it. Once you settle in, focus a soft gaze on one crystal (or other object if you are not using crystals) as you contemplate one aspect of your meditation. Shift your gaze to the next petal or sector when you are ready to move your thoughts to another aspect. Continue until you have worked around to each petal and each part of your meditation. When you have done this, close your eyes and visualize six petals of energy connecting the sectors on the altar as each part of your meditation comes together in completion. Hold this for as long as it seems appropriate and then end your meditation.

The Star

The six-pointed star is commonly called the Star of David or the Magen David. However, this star predates Judaism and has been used as a symbol in many cultures. For example, it is a symbol of the fourth (heart) chakra, and it is through the heart center that we connect with the Divine. It also illustrates the interconnected cycle of creation (Vishnu) and destruction (Shiva).[11] This star has also been called "the creator's star."[12]

The six-pointed star is formed by interlacing two triangles: one pointing up and the other pointing down. Separately, these triangles represent masculine energy (pointing up, the symbol of the vital life force, the blade) and feminine energy (pointing down, the symbol of the pubic triangle and fertility, the chalice). When joined into a star, they represent a balance of energy—yin and yang—and the sacred union of the Goddess and God.

According to Anodea Judith, these intersecting triangles represent "the descent of spirit into the body and the ascent of matter rising to meet spirit."[13] The six-pointed star is also considered to be a joining of the four triangular symbols of the elements. As such, it can relate to the cardinal directions and include the directions "above" and "below."

The star can also represent the lower and higher self. As previously mentioned, the star itself is a symbol of the heart center, which connects

---

11 Annemarie Schimmel, *The Mystery of Numbers*, 125.

12 F. R. Webber, *Church Symbolism*, 52.

13 Anodea Judith, *The Wheels of Life*, 213.

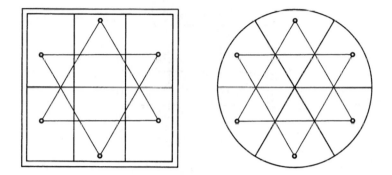

Figure 6.4—A six-pointed star matrix is easy to create on a round or square table.

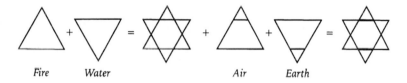

Fire   *Water*   *Air*   *Earth*

Figure 6.5—The four elements as six-pointed star.

the lower and upper chakras and is the source that shares divine energy. In Western cultures, we think of the heart as being the seat of our souls.

If you are familiar with the chakra system, you may want to use additional related symbols. When you begin your meditation, start at the bottom of the star. "I exist" represents the root chakra—survival. "I feel" represents the sacral chakra—the seat of emotions, pleasure, and pain. "I control" is the solar plexus chakra. It represents courage and self-empowerment. "I express" comes from the throat chakra—speak truth and find your focus. "I am the witness" is about insight and realizing that you are the witness to your embodied spirit. "I am that I am" is cosmic consciousness.

As you move through each point of this meditation, maintain awareness that all of these things that you are come from "I love"—your heart. You may find that this evokes a powerful sense of compassion for yourself. Love who you are and then share it with the world.

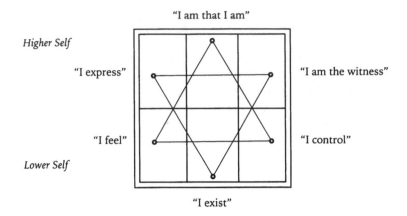

"I am that I am"

Higher Self

"I express"   "I am the witness"

"I feel"   "I control"

Lower Self

"I exist"

Figure 6.6—Unifying higher and lower self.

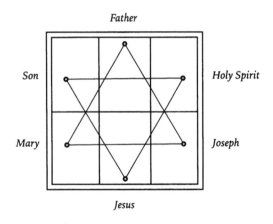

Father

Son   Holy Spirit

Mary   Joseph

Jesus

Figure 6.7—A Christian meditation.

Figure 6.7 illustrates a Christian perspective for a six-part meditation.

The Hexagon

There are many other groupings of six that can be used for meditation. Following are a few additional suggestions. You can visualize a simple hexagon on the six-part altar for any application of six.

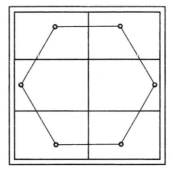

Figure 6.8—A simple hexagon altar layout using gemstones or crystals.

Six symbolizes the stages of planetary evolution: mineral, vegetable, animal, human, angelic, and the unknowable mystery of the Divine.[14] When you set up your altar for this, any symbol or object that resonates for you can represent the Divine. However, in the spirit of this meditation, the Divine is unknowable, and you might want to leave an empty space at the sixth point and allow your mind to contemplate this. I originally thought of making this a six-pointed star meditation (the Divine being at the top point), but a more circular and equal pattern appealed to me, since I believe that everyone and everything has a right to exist. As with the other meditations in this book, follow what is in your heart.

The Tibetan wheel of life consists of six sectors. These are variously referred to as the six states of existence, the six roads to reincarnation, and the six realms of *samsara*. This is a Buddhist concept that is based on the Hindu philosophy of samsara, the cycle of conditioned experiences. Table 6.3 contains the basic attributes of each sector. Different sources switch stages four and five; as always, follow your intuition. If you are not familiar with this, it can at first glance seem like a rather dismal idea for meditation. However, viewing the world or the self through rose-colored glasses does not bring about change and growth. Acknowledging suffering

---

14 Dr. Lauren Artress, *Walking a Sacred Path*, 60. Dr. Artress uses these as the symbols for the six lobes of the labyrinth center.

TABLE 6.3—SIX STATES OF EXISTENCE

State	Characterized by
1. Being in hell	Anger, aggression
2. Hungry ghosts	Desire, cravings, and starvation
3. Animal	Ignorance, servitude
4. Human	Distracting emotions, good and evil—stage of choice
5. Asura (demigods)	Jealousy
6. Deva (heavenly beings)	Pride

in the world and personal suffering can help us grow more compassionate and move forward to something better.

Finally, the following meditation can be used to keep you well grounded on the physical plane and bring you fully into your body. The Ayurvedic system, which originated in India over three thousand years ago, recognizes six tastes: sweet, salty, sour, pungent (spicy), bitter, and astringent. When used in proper amounts, they bring the three *doshas* (fundamental energies) of the body into balance.[15] Table 6.4 lists the types of things that can be used. Place a little of each on a small dish in each sector.

The order in which you place them and taste them is up to you. You will only need a tiny amount to place on your tongue. As in the five senses meditation, allow yourself time to fully experience each taste, and be aware of any feelings or memories they evoke. When you have finished all six, close your eyes and allow yourself to drift into a deep sense of connection with your physical body. Consider the combinations of basic elements that are associated with each taste, as well as other associations, including memories that may arise in response to the tastes. Bringing harmony to the physical energies aids in bringing body, mind, and spirit into balance.

---

15 Vasant Lad, *The Complete Book of Ayurvedic Home Remedies*, 96.

TABLE 6.4—GUIDE TO TYPES OF TASTE ACCORDING TO AYURVEDIC PRINCIPLES

Taste	Foods	Elements	Aspects
Sweet	Fruits, dairy, nuts	Earth & water	Increases vital essence of life
Salty	Table salt, seaweed	Water & fire	Promotes growth
Sour	Pickles, acidic fruits	Earth & fire	Energizes body, nourishes heart
Pungent	Mustard, ginger	Fire & air	Clarity of perception
Bitter	Dandelion, endive, chicory	Air & space	Cooling, lightness
Astringent	Nutmeg, rosehips	Air & earth	Healing

Ram Das says that being mindful when eating keeps us grounded on an experiential level.[16]

List of Correspondences for the Number Six

Astrology: Gemini, Sun, Venus, Virgo

Colors: Indigo, pink, turquoise

Day of the week: Friday

Elements: Air, earth

Energy: Feminine

Gemstones: Amber, carnelian, diamond, pearl, quartz, sapphire, topaz

Message: "I comfort"

Month: June

Pythagorean name: Hexad

Rune: Norse Kaun, Anglo-Saxon Cen

Tarot: The Lovers

---

16 Ram Das, *Paths to God*, 288.

The Seven-Part Altar

The Number Seven

Seven encompasses the cardinal directions and the center, as well as above and below. It is a melding of the four elements with the three realms (heaven, earth, underworld). Medieval scholars viewed seven as a combination of the mundane (four, the material world) and the holy (three, the spiritual world).[1] Seven is the number symbolic of bringing all things into existence, as well as change. To the ancient Egyptians, the number seven was a symbol of eternal life as well as a complete cycle. In traditional Chinese medicine, *qi qing* are the seven affects—emotional or mental states that are potential precursors to disease: anger, anxiety, fright, excessive joy, melancholy, sorrow, and terror.[2]

Because according to the Bible, God made the world in six days and rested on the seventh; seven has long been considered sacred. The Virgin Mary is sometimes depicted with a crown of seven stars. In the Book of Revelation, there are seven stars, seven spirits before God, seven plagues, seven angels that open the seven seals, and seven trumpets that sound.[3] The Gnostics believed in seven levels of understanding; levels eight and nine were akin to reaching nirvana.[4]

---

1 John H. Conway and Richard K. Guy, *The Book of Numbers*, 68.

2 Sandy Fritz, *Mosby's Fundamentals of Therapeutic Massage*, 484.

3 John H. Conway and Richard K. Guy, *The Book of Numbers*, 69.

4 Elaine Pagels, *The Gnostic Gospels*, 136.

There are seven days to the week, seven major chakras, seven visible colors in a rainbow, and seven possible crystalline structures. Each of the four lunar phases consists of seven days. There is an age-old belief from many cultures that humans pass through seven stages of development.[5] Plato and the Hindus described "man" as having seven bodies: physical, ethereal, emotional, causal, mental, divine spirit, and divine vitality.

In Jaina cosmology, the earth was divided into seven equal parts.[6] Medieval alchemists worked with seven metals: copper, gold, iron, lead, mercury, silver, and tin.

Seven has been perceived as a lucky number and one that brings gifts. The seventh son of a seventh son was believed to have special talents. There are seven tones in an octave and seven musical keys. Rome was built on seven hills. Buddha was said to have walked around the bodhi tree seven times before sitting down to meditate.[7]

Basic Associations

abundance	introspection	security
bliss	intuition	spirituality
completion	other worldly realms	stability
endurance	perfection	
freedom	rest	

Using the Seven-Part Altar

The Chakras

Accessing the chakras is a powerful way to work with your energy. The first four correspond to the four elements and can provide a method for balancing these archetypal energies as well as come into balance with the natural world around you in a four-part meditation. The first three chakras are very

---

5 Annemarie Schimmel, *The Mystery of Numbers*, 129.

6 John McLeish, *Number*, 18.

7 Annemarie Schimmel, *The Mystery of Numbers*, 152.

"self" oriented and form the basis of our instincts about survival, sexuality, and courage. When we add the fourth chakra, the heart, our energy begins to move out of these basic needs and into the world. It is the fourth chakra that balances the three lower ones, our foundation, with the three higher ones, which are centered on expression, intuition, and spirituality.

The attributes of all seven chakras are as follows:

The first chakra, the root chakra, is our taproot. It is what keeps us grounded, and the experience it brings us is survival. It is about subsistence and security. Its message is "I exist." It is the seat of our fears, and if our energy gets stuck here, we live in fear. Activating and moving this energy up to the other chakras gives us a stable foundation.

The second chakra, the sacral chakra, is the seat of our emotions. The experience it brings is sensuality and procreation. It is about needs and desires. It gives us the capacity to feel both pleasure and pain. Its message is "I feel." If our energy gets stuck here, we can easily become addicted to things. Activating and moving this energy stokes our creativity.

The third chakra, the solar plexus chakra, is our center of power and control. The experience it brings us is strength and courage. It is the seat of our will. Its message is "I control." From it, we are self empowered; stuck here, we can become overpowering to others. Activating and moving this energy allows us to share our power and courage for the common good of all.

The fourth chakra, the heart chakra, is our place of love and compassion. The experience it brings is acceptance of all life as well as trust. From it, we can be free from expectations and judgment. Its message is "I love." Activating and moving this energy, we share our love and compassion with others and, equally important, we feel these for ourselves.

The fifth chakra, the throat chakra, is our means for communicating with the world. The experience it brings is to share our inner world with others and ask for what we want. From it, we speak our truth. Its message is "I express." Activating and moving this energy allows us to take part in community and share our gifts.

Crown
Third eye
Throat
Heart
Solar plexus
Sacral
Root

Figure 7.1—The seven chakras altar matrix.

The sixth chakra, the third-eye chakra, is our awareness. The experience it brings is insight. From it, we can be objective about ourselves and everything around us. Its message is "I am the witness." Activating and moving this energy awakens intuition, allowing us to "see" with more than our eyes.

The seventh chakra, the crown chakra, is our connection with cosmic consciousness. From it, we can touch Source and know our part in it. Its message is "I am that I am." Activating and moving this energy brings peace and oneness.

Set up your altar with objects, colors, or keywords printed on paper. Each chakra has two sounds associated with it: the seed sound that activates the energy and the vowel sound that moves the energy out of the chakra. Begin with the root chakra and proceed up through them, chanting the following seed sounds: LAM, VAM, RAM, YAM, HAM, OM, OM. The difference between "OM" in chakras six and seven is that the former is brief (just say, "OM") and the latter is sustained (the eternal "AUM" sound).

Take a few moments to think about the aspects or qualities of each chakra as you chant its corresponding sound. Once you have chanted the seed sounds, begin at the root again and chant the vowel sounds to move the energy upward from one chakra to the next as you move supported from your foundation into passion, into strength, and then into compas-

TABLE 7.1—ASPECTS AND ASSOCIATIONS OF THE CHAKRAS

Chakra	Location	Focus	Self	Symbol	Actual color	Emanating color	Bij/seed sound (pronunciation)	Mantra/vowel sound
1st: Root	Base of spine	Survival, grounding	Preservation	Bright yellow square	Deep red	Red	LAM (LUM)	OH (as in *throw*)
2nd: Sacral	One inch below the navel	Sexuality, emotions, desires	Gratification	White crescent moon	Reddish orange	Orange	VAM (VUM)	OO (as in *boo*)
3rd: Solar plexus	The stomach area	Power, will, courage	Definition	Deep red triangle	Dark gray	Yellow	RAM (RUM)	AH (as in *father*)
4th: Heart	The heart center	Love, compassion, relationships	Acceptance	Smoky gray hexagon	Golden	Green	YAM (YUM)	AY (as in *play*)
5th: Throat	Throat	Communication	Expression	White circle	Purple	Blue	HAM (HUM)	EE (as in *see*)
6th: Third eye	Between the eyebrows	Intuition, imagination	Reflection	White lingam	White	Violet	OM (OM)	MM (as in *hum*)
7th: Crown	Crown of the head	Awareness, consciousness	Knowledge	Beyond symbols	White	White	OM (OOMM)	ENC (as in *English*)

sion and on. Do this slowly and multiple times to have an opportunity to experience any shift in energy levels. Once you feel this, continue chanting the eternal "OM," or if it feels more appropriate, chant "AY" to send your love and compassion out to the world. When it feels appropriate, cease chanting and sit in silence. Take time to simply be in your experience. Again, when it feels appropriate to you, chant the vowel sounds in descending order, ending with several "OHs" to ground your energy.

The Star

The seven-pointed star is called a heptagram or septagram—both *hept-* and *sept-* mean "seven." This star is also known as the faery or elven star, witch's star, astrologer's star, and the star of the seven sisters (the Pleiades). It is a star that has three points above the middle and four below.

To Native American people and Neopagans, the points represent seven directions: the four cardinal directions, zenith/above, nadir/below, and here/center/inward.[8] This star creates a circle and sphere of energy for meditation that helps us move inward to get in touch with our inner self.

As the faery star, its sectors represent the four cities and gifts brought by the Tuatha Dé Danann (see "The Four-Part Altar") and the three Celtic realms of sky, sea, and earth. The points of the star represent honor, truth, justice, service, faith, hope, and love.

In meditation, the four sectors below the midline represent the four elements of the physical world. The three above can represent the Christian Trinity, the aspects of the Goddess, or another triple deity. Overall, it is symbolic of spirit embodied in the world. If a "heaven and earth" meditation appeals to you, set up your altar with objects or keywords on paper that have meaning for you. As in other meditations, take your time and focus on each sector as long as necessary. At the end, give yourself time to assimilate the altar as a whole.

Seven-part Christian prayers, usually said with the rosary, can be used for meditation with this altar setup. One is the seven graces granted by

---

8 E. Barrie Kavasch, *The Medicine Wheel*, 25.

Spiritual
Heavenly plane

Physical
Earthly plane

Figure 7.2—The seven-pointed star.

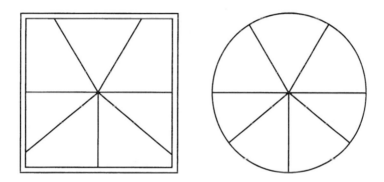

Figure 7.3—The seven-pointed star altar layout.

Mary to those who honor her daily. This devotion is said to have been passed on by Saint Brigit. Another is the Seven Gifts of the Holy Spirit: wisdom, understanding, knowledge, counsel, fortitude, piety, and reverence ("fear of the Lord" in the original).[9]

---

9 Michael Glazier and Monika K. Hellwig, *The Modern Catholic Encyclopedia*, 343.

TABLE 7.2—CORRESPONDENCES FOR THE SEVEN PLANETS

Planet	Personal aspect	Gemstones	Symbol
Sun	Soul, willpower	Ruby, red garnet	☉
Venus	Creativity, love, compassion	Diamond, white topaz	♀
Mercury	Wisdom, senses	Emerald, green tourmaline, peridot	☿
Moon	Emotions, imagination	Pearl, moonstone	☽
Saturn	Overall potential	Sapphire, blue spinel, amethyst	♄
Jupiter	Spirituality, philosophy of life	Yellow sapphire, yellow topaz, citrine	♃
Mars	Ambitions, strength, self-confidence	Coral, bloodstone, cornelian	♂

Astrology

The astronomers in Mesopotamia noted "seven wanderers" that moved through the field of fixed stars.[10] These consisted of Mercury, Venus, Mars, Saturn, Jupiter, the sun, and the moon. The concept of seven levels of heaven, or seven heavens, may have come from the fact that there were seven visible "planets." In Christian and Islamic belief as well as Norse and Mayan mythology, the seventh level of heaven was beyond what humans could imagine or describe.

This meditation is another very personal one that helps you focus on self. Moving inward in truth helps us accept who we are. For all our foibles and issues, there is a great deal of good within us. In addition, being able to "shine" in the outer world starts with acknowledging a spark that shines in our inner worlds. Table 7.2 contains a guide to the aspects of self related to each planet and the gemstones that can be used to represent each. Alternatively, the names or astrological symbols can be used. Begin at any point and proceed in the order that feels appropriate for

---

10 W. M. O'Neil, *Early Astronomy from Babylonia to Copernicus*, 8.

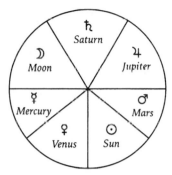

Figure 7.4—The seven ancient "planets" as a wheel.

TABLE 7.3—ALCHEMICAL MEANING OF PLANETARY SYMBOLS

Planet	Symbol	Meaning
Saturn	♄	The body conceals the light of mind and spirit
Jupiter	♃	Spirit emerges from restriction
Mars	♂	The body continues to dominate the mind
Venus	♀	The mind emerges from restriction
Moon	☽	The spirit reflects divine grace
Sun	☉	Divine illumination
Mercury	☿	Balance of body (cross), mind (circle), and spirit (crescent)

you. When you are finished, allow yourself time to sit in silence with the thoughts and feelings that this meditation may evoke.

The altar setup illustrated in Figure 7.4 follows the ancient order of the planets, which indicates the relative orbital velocity of the visible planets beginning with Saturn, the slowest. For your meditation, you may want to begin with the sun, since it represents the soul.

The symbols that we use today for the planets did not originate with the ancient astronomers. It wasn't until the Renaissance in Europe that the planets were assigned symbols with meanings associated with the Greco-Roman gods and goddesses. For example, the circle with a dot for the sun represented the wheels of Helios's celestial chariot. The actual symbols were a product of alchemy, in which each planet was associated with a metal. The alchemical meanings ascribed to these symbols can serve as the basis for self-contemplation.

Astrology and the Chakras

The chakras are also associated with these planets as well as the twelve signs of the zodiac. After all, we are "star stuff." Some of these associations have variants, as shown by the double columns in Table 7.4. As you may have discovered by now, I am a strong believer in personal interpretation. Because of this, I think that the manner in which astrology and the chakras are applied for this type of meditation is a personal matter. Use Table 7.4 and Figure 7.5 as guides or starting points for your own workings.

Descent into Self

Just as some people believed that there were seven levels to heaven, so too was it thought that the underworld contained the same number of levels. This is common throughout a number of cultures. In ancient Egypt, it was believed that there were seven gates that led to seven great halls in the underworld, which was also known as the kingdom of Osiris. Each of these gates was guarded by a doorkeeper, a herald, and a watcher. Before being allowed to pass, a person had to appease all three.[11] Similarly, the cave of Mithras was said to have seven doors. These doors or gates and the challenges issued to those wishing to enter are representative of rites of initiation. Ancient mystery schools, such as the cult of Mithras, required seven degrees of initiation.[12]

---

11 E. A. Wallis Budge, *Egyptian Magic*, 165.

12 Annemarie Schimmel, *The Mystery of Numbers*, 143.

TABLE 7.4—THE CHAKRAS WITH ASSOCIATED PLANETS AND ZODIAC SIGNS

Chakra	Ancient planets		Zodiac signs	
Crown	Sun	—	Leo	—
Third eye	Moon	Moon, Sun	Cancer	Capricorn, Sagittarius
Throat	Mercury	Mercury	Virgo, Gemini	Aquarius, Scorpio
Heart	Venus	Venus	Libra, Taurus	Pisces, Libra
Solar plexus	Jupiter	Mars	Scorpio, Aries	Aries, Virgo
Sacral	Mars	Jupiter	Sagittarius, Pisces	Taurus, Leo
Root	Saturn	Saturn	Capricorn, Aquarius	Gemini, Cancer

	Crown	☉	
Capricorn	Third eye	☽	Sagittarius
Aquarius	Throat	☿	Scorpio
Pisces	Heart	♀	Libra
Aries	Solar plexus	♂	Virgo
Taurus	Sacral	♃	Leo
Gemini	Root	♄	Cancer

Figure 7.5—The chakras matrix with the seven ancient "planets" and modern zodiac.

One well-known story of an initiatory-like descent is that of the goddess Inanna, who was also known as Ishtar. The story dates from 1900–1600 BCE in the kingdom of Sumer. According to various versions, Inanna descends to the underworld to rescue her beloved Dumuzi, or to take the throne and power of her sister Ereshkigal.[13]

---

13 David Leeming and Jake Page, *Goddess*, 62–66.

121

At the first gate, she surrenders her crown, then a necklace, bracelets, outer robe, shoes, and so on, until at the seventh gate she is stripped of everything. According to David Fontana, in the ritual discarding of garments, clothing represents symbols of ignorance.[14] She is naked physically and metaphorically, because each item she surrendered was symbolic of an aspect of her power. In a sense, this is like working backward through the chakras beginning at the crown and ending at our base—stripped down to the final chakra and the seat of our fears. As Leeming and Page put it, the myth of Inanna speaks of the important necessity of confronting and assimilating what has been labeled our dark side before self-knowledge can become complete.[15]

Recreating this kind of descent for a meditation can be a difficult challenge, but it doesn't have to be. When doing self work, it is helpful to strip away the illusions we hold about ourselves. Give it some thought and then choose seven things by which you define yourself. It could be the town or area where you live, the profession you practice, a spiritual path, or a particular club or organization to which you belong. Try also to include things on the personal level, such as the way you dress or wear your hair or the type of car you drive, if these are things that are an important part of your self-image.

Once you have seven aspects to work with, use objects to represent them or write keywords on slips of paper, and place these in the seven sectors of your altar. One by one, think of each and what it would be like not to have this affiliation. When you have stripped away these things from the image you hold of yourself, examine who you are underneath. Who is the person at your core? Allow yourself time to sit in this new place and absorb the essence of true self.

This is not an easy meditation, because we learn from a very early age to identify with "things" that are outside of self. In our over-busy lives, we rarely take time to be quiet with ourselves. We have little opportunity

---

14 David Fontana, *The Meditator's Handbook*, 172.

15 David Leeming and Jake Page, *Goddess*, 61.

to find out who we really are. However, once we find that kernel of self, we usually begin to discover a new way of being in the world and with ourselves.

Days of the Week

A "seven" that we live with constantly is the days of the week. There are a couple of versions as to why most calendars settled on a seven-day week. One reason given is that it accommodated the cycle of the moon. Every seven days, the moon passes into one of its four major phases: new, first quarter, full, and third quarter. Another explanation of the seven-day week is that one day was given over to honor each of the seven known planets and the gods or goddesses that they represented. This latter reason seems most plausible in view of the names of the days. While many of the names originated with the ancient Romans, in English many are derived from the Norse pantheon.

Each day of the week has various associations, and so instead of just meditating on the deity for whom the day was named, focusing on something that corresponds to the day is more useful. This meditation could actually be used for a weeklong theme by concentrating on the associations of the current day.

Set up your altar with objects or keywords in either a linear or circular pattern. A circular or seven-star setup can be effective for relating to

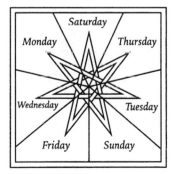

Figure 7.6—The star altar setup is based on the ancient order of the planets.

TABLE 7.5—CORRESPONDENCES FOR THE DAYS OF THE WEEK

	Monday	Tuesday	Wednesday	Thursday	Friday	Saturday	Sunday
Attributes	Family, intuition, spirituality, travel	Courage, challenges, action, strength	Balance, communication, creativity, learning	Giving, growth, health, wealth	Arts, love, passions, peace	Cast away, unwanted, cleansing, protection	Healing, abundance, personal goals
Color	White, silver	Red	Green, orange	Purple, blue	Pink, sky blue	Black, brown	Orange, yellow
Metal	Silver	Iron	Quicksilver, platinum	Tin	Copper	Lead	Gold
Angel	Gabriel	Samuel	Raphael	Sachiel	Ariel	Cassiel	Michael
Gemstone	Moonstone, pearl	Ruby, bloodstone	Aventurine, sodalite	Amethyst, turquoise	Rose quartz, jade	Jet, obsidian	Carnelian, amber

time in a cyclical rather than linear fashion. However, the linear layout can provide a sense of moving forward, especially if you start your meditation on a Sunday or Monday and make that the first sector on the altar. Either way is equally effective. The seven-star setup is based on the ancient order of planets. Following the lines of the star creates the weekly order of days.

With either altar setup, where you place each day is a personal decision. If you are doing this meditation over a week's time, you may want to place only those objects or a keyword for the current day, leaving the others bare. The presence of the other sectors holds the intent while emphasizing the focus on "today." Table 7.5 contains a listing of suggested correspondences. If you have other associations for each day, use whatever has greater meaning for you.

List of Correspondences for the Number Seven

Astrology: Jupiter, Libra, Mercury, Neptune, Venus
Colors: Gold, purple, silver, violet
Day of the week: Saturday
Element: Water
Energy: Masculine
Gemstones: Amethyst, aquamarine, azurite, emerald, jade, lapis lazuli
Message: "I seek"
Month: July
Pythagorean name: Heptad
Rune: Ehwaz
Tarot: Chariot

The Eight-Part Altar

The Number Eight

In ancient Egypt and Babylonia, the solar disk was often depicted with eight rays; an eighth level of existence was beyond the seven planetary spheres and represented the domain of the gods.[1] The goddess Inanna/Ishtar was associated with the astral symbol of an eight-pointed star.[2] An eight-petalled lotus symbolizes luck and beauty, and its petals represent material nature: air, earth, fire, water, ether, mind, intellect, and ego-sense.

Norse god Odin's horse is depicted with eight legs, symbolizing swiftness as well as the division of the year into eight parts.[3] The Pagan Wheel of the Year is turned by eight annual festivals that mark changing points in the year and are accompanied by a shift in energy.

In some practices, eight major chakras are acknowledged, with a soul chakra located in the etheric body approximately two or three inches above the head. Among other things, Buddhist mandalas symbolize the Eightfold Path. Eight trigrams of the *I Ching* are used on an octagon called the *bagua*. The trigrams represent eight fundamental conditions or situations in life.[4]

---

1 Annemarie Schimmel, *The Mystery of Numbers*, 156.

2 Clare Gibson, *Goddess Symbols*, 22.

3 John H. Conway and Richard K. Guy, *The Book of Numbers*, 72.

4 Jami Lin, *The Feng Shui Anthology*, 41–43.

Eight's geometric shape is the octagon, which is a common shape for baptismal fonts in Christian churches because eight is the symbol of life after baptism (rebirth/resurrection). The octagon has been noted as the shape that is between the circle and the square. It combines the four cardinal directions and the cyclical seasons of the earth.

Eight is also considered the number sacred to the concept of rebirth, because following the seven stages of initiation, a person is transformed and reborn into this world or a new world on a higher level. The ancient Chinese believed that humans had eight stages of development.[5]

In the *Yoga Sutras*, Patanjali describes eight limbs of yoga (*ashtanga*), which are basically guidelines on how to live a meaningful life.[6]

Basic Associations

achievement	intellect	spiritual rebirth/
balance	justice	regeneration
confidence	life	strength
fertility	manifestation	totality
foundation	power	
infinity	prosperity	

Using the Eight-Part Altar

The Buddhist Eightfold Path

The Eightfold Path consists of guidelines of practice that bring the teachings of the Four Noble Truths to life. (See "The Four-Part Altar" for the Four Noble Truths.) This practice can help us free ourselves from attachments and delusions (with which modern life is rife) to end suffering and ultimately reach nirvana. Whether or not nirvana is our goal, breaking the shackles of stress is a byproduct that many of us welcome. The word "right" is generally used in designating each aspect of the path;

---

5 Annemarie Schimmel, *The Mystery of Numbers*, 159–160.

6 Sri Swami Satchidananda, *The Yoga Sutras of Patanjali*, 124.

however, this is translated from the Pali word *samma*, which can also be interpreted as "perfect" or "correct."[7]

The eight points are not necessarily steps that need to be followed in sequence. They are separate yet interdependent principles that work in unison. The Four Noble Truths are basically the doctrine, while the Eightfold Path is the practice. According to Lama Surya Das, the eightfold path helps to "develop the three essential values of Buddhism: wisdom, ethics and meditative awareness."[8]

The eight points are as follows:

1. *Right View or Vision.* This means to have an understanding of the Four Noble Truths. Right View is also the ability to see things as they truly are—to "grok" them.[9] It is about developing clear vision that is not clouded by superficial fluff.

2. *Right Intention.* Intention in general is the first step to manifesting anything into the physical world. It focuses our mental energy and leads our actions. Right Intention is a commitment to direct our energy for an ethical and wholesome way of being in the world.[10]

3. *Right Speech.* Right Speech is one form of ethical and wholesome conduct. Words are powerful: they can do great good or harm. Right Speech means to avoid deliberate lies and deceitfulness, to not slander others or cause pain with our words, and to avoid gossip (speech that lacks purpose). It is about speaking the truth.

4. *Right Action.* This is another form of ethical and wholesome conduct. It means to avoid intentionally harming others. It also means to not take what is not given. It is the resolve to act with kindness, honesty, and compassion out of respect for others.

---

7 Kulananda, *Principles of Buddhism*, 21.

8 Lama Surya Das, *Awakening the Buddha*, 93.

9 The word *grok* was invented by Robert Heinlein in his book *Stranger in a Strange Land* (New York: Putnam, 1963). It means to have a profound understanding of something not only through intellect but also intuition and empathy.

10 *Wholesome* here refers specifically to nonviolence and mindfulness.

5. *Right Livelihood.* Right Livelihood means that we make our living through means that are legal and peaceful. In our world of multi-national conglomerates, it is important to look beyond our immediate places of business to understand the full impact of whatever industry we have a part in.

6. *Right Effort.* Effort is acting from the will, which can be misguided if we are not mindful. This concerns having passion for what we do and how we live our lives.

7. *Right Mindfulness or Awareness.* This is based on clear perception and self-awareness. It means to be aware of what we do and the effects of the actions that ripple out from us.

8. *Right Concentration.* Concentration is one-pointedness of the mind. In this case, it is directed toward ethical and wholesome thoughts and actions. Through meditation and contemplation, this can eventually become second nature in our everyday lives.

Set up your altar in either format illustrated in Figure 8.1. Keywords may be easier to use unless particular objects clearly define each of the eight parts of the path to you. As previously mentioned, these are not steps that have to be followed in order from one to eight. Begin wherever you feel drawn to start and proceed in any order that has meaning

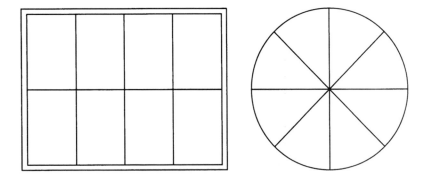

Figure 8.1—Two formats for an eight-part altar.

for you. As you ponder each of the eight parts, note how you may already be practicing them as well as where you want to put more effort.

Keep in mind that this is a *path* and not a test to evaluate whether or not you are a good person. The only evaluation that counts is the one for and by you, done in a compassionate way to help yourself. Examining each point on this path serves to remind us that we are human and are aware of the power that we each hold to help or hinder ourselves and others.

Eight Auspicious Symbols

Although of pre-Buddhist origin, the Tibetan Buddhist symbols known in Sanskrit as *Ashtamangala*, or eight (*ashta*) auspicious (*mangala*) symbols, represented gifts from the Vedic gods when the Shakyamuni Buddha attained enlightenment.[11] These were said to have been gifts bestowed by celestial beings. They have been used in art as powerful signs associated with the body of Buddha as well as on their own as an embodiment of the entire cosmos. The symbols are used on sacred and secular objects, carpets, furniture, metalwork, and silk brocade. In ceremonies, they are frequently created on the ground by sprinkling colored flour. The use of these symbols is believed to bring happiness and protection.

The meaning of the symbols are as follows:

The *conch* is considered to be the original trumpet (perhaps along with the ram's horn), and it is the main emblem of Vishnu. It is a symbol of power, authority, and sovereignty. In the Hindu *Bhagavad Gita*, the great warrior Arjuna had a conch (as all warriors did) and used it like a bugle to signal the commencement of battle. Blowing the conch was also believed to banish evil spirits and chase away poisonous creatures. Tibetan Buddhists sound a conch to call people together for worship. It is also used in ritual as a vessel for holy water. Conchs that spiral to the right are rare and considered sacred. This clockwise spiral is associated with the movement of celestial bodies and called deosil or sunwise motion. Like the

---

11 Robert Beer, *The Handbook of Tibetan Buddhist Symbols*, 1.

TABLE 8.1—CORRESPONDING DIRECTIONS OF THE EIGHT AUSPICIOUS SYMBOLS

Symbol	Name	Direction
	Conch	North
	Vase	Northeast
	Umbrella	East
	Lotus	Southeast
	Banner	South
	Fish	Southwest
	Endless knot	West
	Wheel	Northwest

resonant sound that carries a distance from the conch, it symbolizes the far-reaching music of dharma teachings.

The *treasure vase* represents long life, abundance, prosperity, and all good things for life on earth as well as liberation from physical life. The vase is said to remain perpetually full no matter how much is removed from it. Its presence is believed to attract wealth and harmony. Above all, the vase symbolizes the spiritual abundance of the Buddha, which never ran out no matter how much he gave away to others.

The *umbrella* or *parasol* represents the dome of the sky, with the function of casting a protective shadow that shields us from suffering and harmful forces. It creates a cool shade in which life is preserved from parching defilements. In some cultures, it was a symbol of status to be protected from the elements, especially if the umbrella was held by someone else. Holding it above someone's head represented respect and honor. Metaphorically, the handle is the *axis mundi*, which also represents spiritual support. The dome represents wisdom, and the hanging skirt, compassion.

The *lotus* does not grow in Tibet, and as a result, depictions of it are stylized rather than realistic. All important Buddhist deities are in some way associated with or pictured with the lotus. With its roots in the mud, stem in the water, and flower open to the heavens, the lotus is symbolic of spiritual growth. mud represents the earthly physical realm, water the emotions and experiences of life, and the flower the crowning achievement of enlightenment. As a whole, it represents transcending the body and the materialistic desires of the world and blossoming into the bliss of liberation.

The *banner*, or victory banner, is an emblem of Buddha's enlightenment, which is the triumph of wisdom over ignorance. It also represents the ability to overcome the obstacles we encounter along our paths. In addition, it symbolizes the small, everyday victories we can celebrate by staying with our practices.

Two golden fish facing each other is an ancient symbol (pre-Buddhist) that represented the two major rivers of India: the Ganga and Yamuna. These rivers represent solar and lunar energy flowing through the land just as they flow through our bodies in the *ida* and *pingala* channels that crisscross our spines. (Refer to "The Three-Part Altar" for more information on these.) The golden fish symbolize abundance as well as a fearless freedom to swim through the challenging oceans of life.

The intertwining lines of the *endless knot* represent the interconnectedness of all things. It is a symbol of harmony and balance. The knot is a reminder of how we are bound to our karmic destiny. With no beginning or ending, it symbolizes the great wisdom of the Buddha. (To my Irish eyes, it looks very Celtic.)

The *wheel*, a circle, is a symbol of perfection in many cultures. The hub represents the world's axis as well as training in moral discipline. It is the stabilizer and support of the mind. The eight spokes of the wheel represent the Eightfold Path that leads to the end of suffering. This occurs with the right application of wisdom gained from training and practice in moral discipline. The rim of the wheel represents the concentration that holds it all together, helping us stay in our practices and on our paths. It is also called the wheel of transformation, the motion being a symbol of how rapidly the Buddha's teachings can bring about change. His initial instruction became known as "the first turning of the wheel of dharma."

Set up your altar with pictures or keywords representing the eight auspicious symbols in sectors corresponding to the directions listed in Table 8.1. Begin with whichever sector or symbol seems appropriate for you. Take time with each sector. As with all meditations presented in this book, add your beliefs to make the experience deeply personal.

The Moon

It is easy for us to flick a switch and have light any time we want. Now, try to imagine what it was like in the time before this convenience and how important moonlight would have been in a world that could be very dark once the sun set. It is no surprise that our ancestors would have been in tune with the cycle of the moon. Even with all of our conveniences, we can still feel the special energy of moonsheen.

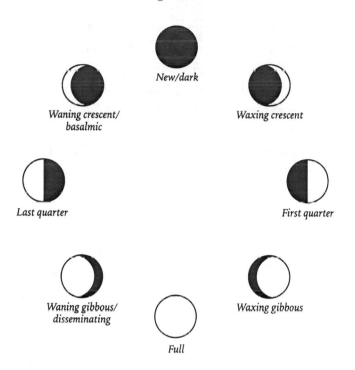

Figure 8.2—The eight lunar phases.

Moonlight has the power to enchant us. To walk in the moonlight is to feel a touch of magic—we cannot help but sense the energy. Luna does not give us a harsh, bright light, as does the sun. She provides just enough to part the darkness of night and invite us into other realms.

Our ancestors planned particular events around the moon phases. The *Farmers' Almanac* still advises on the best time to coordinate planting and harvesting. Over time, familiarize yourself with the moon's cycle so that on any given day you have a sense of which of the eight phases the moon resides in. As you do this, begin to equate events or cycles in your life. Observe what is going on and then see if it might coincide with the moon's cycle. If these cycles are not in sync with the moon, at least note if they follow a lunar pattern.

A moon phase meditation can take place on eight occasions over a month or at one sitting. If anything, it will help you get in tune with the natural cycles while learning to observe life as a cyclical flow. Real-life events and emotions do not begin and end like a movie. Instead, they flow and unfold or ebb to be reworked at a new cycle. Give thought to an issue in your life. Don't try to force a conclusion—just observe its course. The next step is to perceive it according to moon phases. It does not have to be coordinated with the moon itself.

Set up an eight-part altar in a circular format. Place a drawing or photocopy from Figure 8.2 of each moon phase in a sector of the altar. Items that hold meaning for you, runes, or other objects can also be used. Consider your issue in terms of these phases. What was its beginning? When did you become aware of it and how did it manifest itself? Even if it has not reached its "full moon" stage, how might it come to fruition?

If it is a difficult issue that could be negative when it comes to fruition, consider how it could reach fullness in such a way that it could bring about a positive or at least nondestructive outcome. Once it reaches fullness, see it resolved.

Alternatively, now may not be the time for this particular issue to be resolved. Know that it is okay for this to occur, and visualize its ebb. Perhaps bringing it close to a climax is all that is needed to be able to let it dissolve and then let it go. The act of following its potential progression may be enough to let you see that you can rid yourself of a problem and make way for other things in your life.

Visualizing an issue through this cycle can help you get a fresh perspective on it and deal with it when it does occur. Sometimes things may need to run the cycle a few times before reaching their natural end. With this meditation, we can shepherd issues into constructive cycles of changes.

This meditation does not have to deal only with issues that you want to resolve. You could use it as a pattern to observe something occurring in your life, such as college and preparing to make your way in the world, or creative pursuits. Alternatively, it can provide a new way for you to observe the events of your life.

TABLE 8.2—MOON PHASE CORRESPONDENCES

Phase	Attributes	Expressed as	Runes	Goddesses
New/dark	Beginnings, incubation	Turn inward to allow your soul space to create	Fehu, Gebo, Isa, Raido, Uruz	Artemis/Diana, Cerridwen, Hecate, Lucina
Waxing crescent	Quickening, awakening	Stirrings below the surface of consciousness	Berkana, Perth	Brigid, Epona, Exchel
First quarter	Finding a way, manifestation	Whatever needs to develop will come forth	Ansuz, Ehwaz, Jera, Nauthiz	Arianrhod, Artemis/Diana
Waxing gibbous	Moving forward	Patience, a time for fine-tuning	Ansuz, Dagaz, Inguz	Cerridwen, Nut, Ratri
Full	Fruition, sending out	All endeavors culminate	Sowelo, Wunjo	Aimah, Astarte, Hathor, Isamba, Isis, Morrigan
Waning gibbous/disseminating	Breaking off	A time to let go	Hagalaz, Othila, Teiwaz	Hecate, Kali, Luna, Selena, Usas
Last quarter	Clearing out	Accepting endings	Laguz, Teiwaz	Isis, Mert
Waning crescent/basalmic	Making ready	Emptiness, a clean slate upon which your soul will write	Eihwaz, Thurisaz, Uruz	Cerridwen, Eastanatlehi, Inanna, Nasilele

List of Correspondences for the Number Eight

Astrology: Leo, Mercury, Pluto, Saturn, Scorpio, Sun

Colors: Brown, rose, violet

Day of the week: Thursday

Element: Earth

Energy: Feminine

Gemstones: Agate, diamond, opal

Message: "I acquire"

Month: August

Pythagorean name: Ogdoad

Rune: Elhaz

Tarot: Strength

The Nine-Part Altar

The Number Nine

As a product of the sacred number three multiplied by itself (triple trinity), nine represents divine power magnified—the holy of holies that symbolized balance, order, and perfection. The Greeks called it *ennead* and considered it incomplete.[1] In their mythology, the nine muses personified the arts and sciences. Rituals of the Eleusinian Mysteries in ancient Greece lasted for nine days. Odysseus's journey lasted nine years, as did the siege of Troy.[2]

The ancient Chinese believed in nine planes of the sky (the number nine was the symbol of heaven[3]) and that the earth was divided into nine regions.[4] The Maya believed in nine underworlds, with a separate god ruling in each.

In Norse mythology, the World Tree, Yggdrasil, has nine roots, each of which lead to an underworld realm. These were said to exist as three realms on three levels. The Nordic god Odin (a.k.a. Woden) spent nine days and nights suspended upon Yggdrasil in a shamanic quest that yielded knowledge of the runes. He also learned nine sacred songs.[5]

---

1 John H. Conway and Richard K. Guy, *The Book of Numbers*, 74.

2 Annemarie Schimmel, *The Mystery of Numbers*, 164.

3 Ibid., 170.

4 Edward Schafer, *Ancient China*, 102.

5 John H. Conway and Richard K. Guy, *The Book of Numbers*, 74–75.

To Christians, nine is the triple manifestation of the Trinity. There are nine orders of angels in nine levels of heaven and nine orders of demons in nine levels of hell, where nine rivers flowed into the lowest. Chinese and Mexican mythologies also contain nine rivers in the lowest level of the underworld.[6] Islamic cosmology divides the universe into nine spheres.

In the Gospel of Matthew (5:1), Jesus spoke of nine beatitudes in his sermon on the mount. A *novena* is a traditional prayer that is said on nine consecutive days.

According to Richard Rohr and others, there are nine archetypal, universal patterns that create a person's characteristics. Like the three primary colors that are mixed to create all colors, so too are the nine patterns combined into an infinite number of personalities.[7]

There are nine months in human pregnancy, a cat is said to have nine lives, and when you are exceedingly happy, you are on cloud nine. Bringing something to completion is going the whole nine yards, and being perfectly groomed is dressing to the nines.

Basic Associations

change	healing	spirituality
charity	intuition	transformation
compassion	love	wisdom
completion	motion	
generosity	social issues	

Using the Nine-Part Altar

Just as the number nine is perceived as coming full circle, so too are the nine-part altar setups, because they deal with integrating the self. The one-part altar began with the void and singularity, and with nine we come back to center.

---

6 Annemarie Schimmel, *The Mystery of Numbers*, 169.

7 Richard Rohr and Andreas Ebert, *Discovering the Enneagram*, 3–5.

Our lives are so complex and busy that it's far too easy to become fragmented and feel divided or not at home with ourselves. By contemplating the various parts of who we are and our myriad thoughts and emotions, we can come into unified balance with self.

Nine Woods of Sacred Flame

Since ancient times, the tree has served as an important symbol in two ways: as the World Tree, it connected the realms of existence, and as the Tree of Life, it represented the source of life and abundance. Like mythological heroes, trees are larger than life. Their beauty evokes wonder, so it is no surprise that they have long had a central place in folklore, myth, and religion. Their grandeur still serves as a symbol of life, hope, and perseverance.

Trees were also symbols for communities and significant events. In Celtic lands, most tribes had a particular local tree that functioned as their own sacred tree (*crann beatha*) or community talisman.[8] It was a place to gather for important occasions. Likewise, centuries later trees that served as community symbols in Colonial America were called liberty trees and functioned as meeting points in each of the thirteen colonies.

Like the trees themselves, communal fires were important aspects of life—both sacred and secular. Perpetual flames were associated with particular goddesses and served as sources for lighting ritual fires and home hearth flames. Perhaps the two most well-known were dedicated to Vesta (Rome) and Brigid/Saint Brigit (Kildare, Ireland). Perpetual fires were commonly fueled by specific types of wood—for example, oak for Vesta and hawthorn for Brigid.

Some fires, called "need-fires," were kindled for specific purposes, such as rituals, celebrations, and protection.[9] In Tantric ritual, fire is the means by which one is symbolically purified and empowered. Because these fires were not "common" fires, they were kindled using special techniques and

---

8 Peter Berreford Ellis, *The Druids*, 178.

9 Stephen J. Pyne, *Vestal Fire*, 68.

TABLE 9.1—ATTRIBUTES OF THE TREES

Tree	Attribute
Alder	Banishing, divination, foundation, guardian, healing, intuition, protection, rebirth, resurrection, transformation
Apple	Attraction, beauty, faithfulness, fertility, generosity, happiness, harmony, healing, illumination/knowledge, immortality, love, perpetual youth, prosperity, protection, regeneration, choice, strength, wealth
Ash	Ambition, balance, communication, creativity, fertility, growth, healing, illumination/knowledge, love, divination, peace of mind, poetry and storytelling, prophecy, protection (especially from drowning), rebirth, stability, transitions
Aspen	Ancestry, astral projection, communication, courage, eloquence, endurance, harmony, healing, money, peace, protection, rebirth, rejuvenation, success
Birch	Beginnings, birth, blessings, creativity, crafts, fertility, growth, healing, inspiration, love, protection, purification, renewal
Cypress	Healing, longevity, persistence, solace
Elder	Abundance, blessings, consecration, creativity, good fortune, healing, knowledge of magic, positive change, prosperity, protection, sleep, success, transition
Elm	Birth, compassion, empathy, endurance, groundedness, healing, intuition, love, protection, rebirth, stability, wisdom
Fir	Birth, cleverness, farsightedness, protection, prosperity, rebirth, transformation, vitality
Hawthorn	Ancestry, cleansing, defensive protection, family, fertility, growth, happiness, lifts depression, love, luck, marriage, patience, prosperity, protection, purity, reconciliation, wisdom
Hazel	Creativity, divination, fertility, healing, inspiration, introspection, knowledge, luck, marriage, protection, reconciliation, wisdom
Holly	Courage, death, divinity, guidance, healing, intelligence, luck, protection, rebirth, unity
Linden	Attraction, love, luck, peace
Mesquite	Persistence, protection, success
Oak	Ancestry, fertility, healing, health, justice, longevity, loyalty, luck, prosperity, protection, self-confidence, strength, subtlety, success, wisdom, wit
Pine	Abundance, emotions, fertility, good fortune, healing, health, immortality, love, prosperity, protection, purification, regeneration

Tree	Attribute
Rowan	Blessings, centering, dedication, expression, fertility, grounding, healing, imagination, insight, luck, music, poetry, protection, quickening, strength
Walnut	Change, fertility, inspiration, intentions, new perspectives
Willow	Birth, connections, enchantment, fertility, flexibility, healing, intuition (and trusting it), knowledge, protection, relationships, wishes
Yew	Ancestry, change, communication with the dead, death, divinity, flexibility, immortality, longevity, rebirth, strength

certain types of wood. Each type of wood used in a need-fire contributed its special attributes to the health and welfare of the community. It was a frequent practice to extinguish all fires in the village prior to starting the need-fire. Ceremonial flames, bonfires, and all hearth fires were then relit from it.[10]

Like the need-fires, this meditation utilizes the attributes of trees. Begin by selecting nine trees. You may have a strong attachment to particular trees, or simply use the first nine trees that you can think of. Using Table 9.1, look up the associated attributes of your chosen trees. (Also refer to Table 2.4 in "The Two-Part Altar.") Without pausing to analyze them, choose one attribute for each tree and write it on a slip of paper.

Create nine sectors on your altar and then place one of the slips of paper with a tree attribute in each sector. As with your selection of attributes, don't plan where each slip of paper should be placed. Spontaneity in placement as well as which sector you begin with allows the process to unfold naturally.

Prepare for meditation, and when you are ready, pick up one of the slips of paper and focus your attention on the word. Does it have any particular significance in your life at the moment? Whether or not it seems important to your current life situation, note your thoughts and feelings and then move on to the next sector and word. When you have worked

---

10 Ibid., 69.

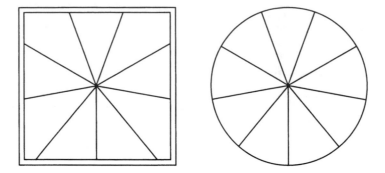

Figure 9.1—The nine-part sacred altar.

with all nine, consider how collectively the words may have greater meaning and currency to you.

Take time to ponder any thought or impression they evoked in you. Journaling your experience lends itself especially well to this meditation, because if you repeat this meditation over time, you may find patterns emerging to the extent that you may be guided by your subconscious or other consciousness to choose certain attributes, even though you don't take time to think about them during the selection process.

The Magic Square

A magic square is a grid with a number in each sector, in which regardless of the direction the numbers are added, the result will be the same. The nine-sector magic square shown in Figure 9.2 contains the numbers 1 to 9 and results in the sum of 15.

The nine-sector magic square in Figure 9.3, called the *Lo Shu grid*, is commonly used in various schools of feng shui. The Lo Shu grid dates to approximately 2205 BCE and was considered by the ancient Chinese to be a "universal model" and was sometimes called the "nine mansions."[11]

---

11 Edward Schafer, *Ancient China*, 102.

4	9	2
3	5	7
8	1	6

Figure 9.2—Regardless of which direction the numbers are added, the result is 15.

4—Southeast	9—South	2—Southwest
Prosperity/abundance	Illumination	Relationships/Part
Self-worth/net worth	Fame/success	Love/romance/marriage
Resources	Reputation/respect	Mother
3—East	**5—Center**	**7—West**
Family	Balance	Creativity
Ancestors	Harmony	Projects
Community		Children
8—Northeast	**1—North**	**6—Northwest**
Wisdom	Career	Achievement/benefactors
Knowledge	Personal journey	Assisting people
Self-cultivation	Foundation	Father

Figure 9.3—The magic square with its attributes.

The feng shui magic square provides a matrix of aspects and correspondences that allows practitioners to work with the energy in their environment and ultimately effect change in their lives. These principles can be applied to a meditation. When you set up your magic square altar (Figure 9.4), you may want to position it with the sectors oriented in their respective directions. Allow intuition to guide you where you should sit. On

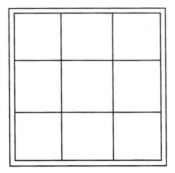

Figure 9.4—The magic square altar matrix.

a slip of paper, write a keyword or two from Figure 9.3, or if something more personal and relevant comes to mind, use that instead of the illustrated keywords. If certain objects are more evocative than keywords, use one for each sector. The center represents self.

I begin this meditation with the east, place of sunrise and brightness, symbolizing new beginnings; however, you can begin with any of the eight outer directions. The meditation can progress in a clockwise or counterclockwise direction, taking time to ponder how each aspect relates to your life. When you have worked your way through the outer eight, focus your attention on the center.

One way of approaching this meditation is to contemplate how these aspects weave together to create your life. Another is to allow the eight outer aspects to fall away as you move to the center, where nothing but true self exists. The ego mind may be tempted to pass judgment. If this occurs, stand firm in a commitment to honor where you are in your life. When you can find happiness with yourself, all other things will fall into place. Accepting and loving who you are right now is what counts.

TABLE 9.2—THE DIRECTIONS AND THEIR ATTRIBUTES

Direction	Attribute
East	Includes all those you love, from your immediate family to the family of humankind, your ancestors, and friends. This is also about growth and vitality.
Southeast	Wealth and abundance on all levels, from self-worth to monetary worth to blessings. Personal resources and anything that enriches your life.
South	To be known in your community or field of employment; to garner respect and recognition. This is concerned with your outward self as well as self-actualization. If you want to shine, work on this area.
Southwest	Encompasses love, romance, marriage, and all types of relationships: personal and business. Many times we learn about relationships through our mothers. This direction is also associated with being receptive.
West	This is about having children, helping children, or stimulating your creative impulses. This is where you nurture all manner of things to which you "give birth."
Northwest	Achievement also includes those who help you achieve: benefactors, mentors, and your father. It is about responsibility—giving as well as receiving.
North	Careers and personal journeys symbolize progress in our lives. Progress is not always about moving forward; at times we must stand still and assess ourselves before we can move onward. Think of this as your area of foundation.
Northeast	Wisdom, knowledge, and self-cultivation also encompass turning points. Gaining self-wisdom can bring about revolutions in our lives.
Center	A place of balance, harmony, and spirituality, this is also considered the prosperity point. To attain balance and harmony requires joy.

The Norse Runes

The runes are sometimes referred to as Odin's alphabet, since he was said to have brought them into the world. According to the Eddas, which recorded Old Norse literature,[12] Odin perceived the runes and their wisdom during a shamanic quest when he suspended himself from Yggdrasil, the World Tree. Runes have been found inscribed on monumental stones throughout Scandinavia as well as in a few other countries. Although their true origin is unknown, they are believed to have been developed in the third century CE.[13] Their use reached its height between the eighth and twelfth centuries in Scandinavian countries.

According to several poems in the Eddas, runes were used as talismans that empowered people and objects, as well as a form of divination. Ralph H. Blum describes them as "akin in function to the Tarot and the Chinese Book of Changes."[14] Whatever their original applications, they are in widespread use today for oracular guidance and meditation.

Of the twenty-four runes, there are nine that cannot be "reversed" because they are the same right-side-up and upside-down. When worked in a pattern, these nine can be a journey of self-discovery. Table 9.3 lists the nine runes, their symbols, and their aspects in the order to follow for this meditation.

Set up your altar in a nine-part grid as illustrated in Figure 9.5 and place the corresponding rune in each sector. For example, Ingwaz goes in sector 1, Dagaz in sector 2. Use a set of rune stones if you have them, or draw the symbol on a piece of paper. (An index card folded in half works well.) Figure 9.5 illustrates two patterns that you can follow in your meditation. One is to begin with the right center sector and work around the outer eight, then end with nine in the middle. The second is to use a

---

12 The *Prose Edda* was recorded by poet-historian Snorri Sturluson circa 1222–1223. The *Poetic Edda* was recorded during the second half of the thirteenth century by unknown authors from material that dates to 800–1100. *Encyclopedia Britannica Micropaedia*, 15th ed., s.v. "The Edda."

13 Ibid., s.v. "Runic Alphabet."

14 Ralph H. Blum, *The Book of Runes*, 20.

TABLE 9.3—RUNIC ASSOCIATIONS

	Name	Symbol	Aspects
1	Ingwaz	ᛜ	Beginnings, balance, bounty
2	Dagaz	ᛗ	Development, happiness, satisfaction
3	Hagalaz	ᚺ	Disruption, change, challenge
4	Nauthiz	ᚾ	Need, necessity, limitation or constraint
5	Isa	ᛁ	Inaction, standstill, reflection, withdrawal
6	Eihwaz	ᛇ	Movement, change, turning point, transformation
7	Jera	ᛃ	Productivity, reaping what you have sewn
8	Gebo	ᚷ	Gift, blessings, partnership/relationship
9	Sowelo	ᛊ	Completion, wholeness, power

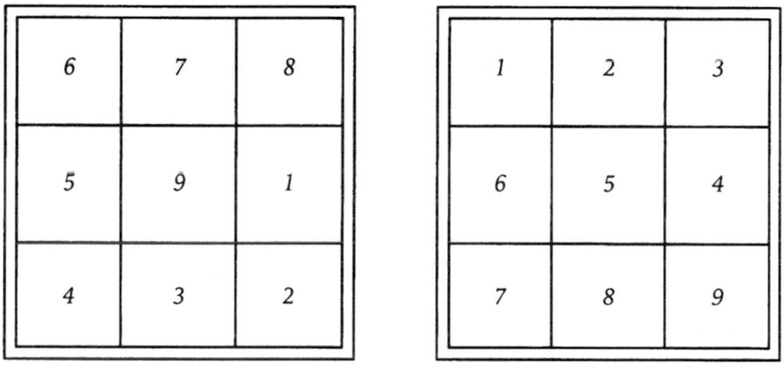

6	7	8
5	9	1
4	3	2

1	2	3
6	5	4
7	8	9

Figure 9.5—Rune meditation patterns.

simple zigzag pattern, beginning with the top left sector and ending with the right bottom. However, if another pattern seems right for you, use it. Likewise, if a round setup seems more appropriate to you, use it.

When you are ready to begin, briefly glance through the runic associations listed in Table 9.3. Don't feel that you have to commit the information to memory, because the mind will find what it needs during the

TABLE 9.4—RUNE PRONUNCIATION

Ingwaz	eng-woz
Dagaz	thaw-gauze
Hagalaz	haw-ga-laws
Nauthiz	now-thees
Isa	ee-saw
Eihwaz	eye-woz
Jera	yare-awe
Gebo	gay-boe
Sowelo	soe-wee-low

meditation. Set the book aside and then gaze at the rune Ingwaz in sector one. Stay with each rune for as long as it feels appropriate.

For an added dimension, you may want to include sound in this meditation. Intoning and chanting are powerful tools for focusing the mind. As you focus on a rune, slowly say, whisper, or sing its name. Table 9.4 provides a pronunciation guide. However, just as there are other ways of spelling the runic names, so too are there alternative ways to pronounce them. If you have learned differently from what is presented here, stay with what you know or give this a try. If you find the sounds particularly effective and would like to carry it further, refer to Edred Thorsson's book *Futhark: A Handbook of Rune Magic.*

As with all other meditations, allow time afterward to journal or simply sit quietly. I find it a good time to linger over a cup of herb tea. Develop your own methods and traditions that will help you maintain your meditation practice.

List of Correspondences for the Number Nine

Astrology: Jupiter, Mars, Moon, Sun, Sagittarius, Virgo

Colors: Indigo, red, yellow

Days of the Week: Monday, Friday

Element: Fire

Energy: Masculine

Gemstones: Aquamarine, bloodstone, clear quartz, garnet, opal, pearl, ruby

Message: "I feel"

Month: September

Pythagorean name: Ennead

Rune: Jera

Tarot: Hermit

In Summary

After working with an altar matrix, you may want to leave it in place so that the visual cues that guided you through the meditation remain as reminders for a day or two. Some altar experiences may be powerful and others less so, but each one will be its own unique journey.

Spiritual practices are rich and varied—one size does not fit all. The way in which people interact with their altars is equally diverse. The purpose of this book is to introduce different altar setups and matrices to help you explore inner and outer (beyond one's self) space. You may want to start with those setups that are in keeping with your religious tradition or cultural heritage and then move on to others. My sense is that there are many more "game boards" that can be developed.

My hope is that using the altar for introspection serves to enrich your spiritual path and deepen your sense of self. In keeping and using an altar, you are participating in an ancient act that is fundamental to humanity. This is a practice that can bring you face to face with the Divine as well as with your true inner soul.

A History of Altars

In order to develop an appreciation for how integral and cross-cultural altars have been, we need to take a look at their history. Because it is beyond the scope of this book, the history presented here is not as inclusive or in-depth as such a study would warrant. However, this brief review provides a window into the past, with "snapshots" from various eras and areas of the world.

The word *altar* evolved from *altare* in Old Frisian (Netherlands and Germany) and *altari* from Old Saxon, Old High German, and Old Norse, which came from the Latin *altāre*. The Latin word *altāria* meant "an altar for burnt offerings." The Latin word *ara* had two meanings: "altar for hearth and home" as well as "a refuge for protection." The Old English world *altar* replaced the native words *wēofod* and *wēobed*, which meant "idol table."[1]

---

1 C. T. Onions, *The Oxford Dictionary of English Etymology*, 28–29, 54.

Paleolithic to Classical Civilizations

The concept of deity emerged at the dawn of human civilization, as did the almost universal belief that divinity was manifest on mountaintops. This was eventually instrumental in the building of great structures to help humans meet the Divine halfway—more or less. The high place or sacred heights could be natural (mountaintop or hilltop) or artificial (raised mound or tall temple).

Wherever human settlements have been discovered, evidence of altars has been found. Altars are as old as human belief in divinity and represent the attempt to communicate with this divine entity. According to Reverend Elaine Farmer, people looked upon deity with "wonder, gratitude or fear." They wanted to make offerings to "honor, thank, appease or cajole" and needed a special place to do it.[2] However, altars were not only intended for communication with a supreme god or goddess, they were also used to maintain contact with ancestors and other spirits.

Although based on speculation, the potentially oldest-known altar dates to approximately 30,000 BCE in France. It was in use around the same time as the famous Lascaux Cave; however, in Chauvet Cave, a bear skull was placed on a flat-topped rock in the middle of one of the chambers. The rock is roughly two feet square and about two feet high. Small chunks of charcoal were scattered on the top of the rock and were also found underneath the bear skull. The skull was aesthetically oriented on the rock and perched with the front of its upper jaw hanging over the edge of the rock. Dr. Jean Clottes, an archaeologist and a science advisor to France's Ministry of Culture, noted that bears hibernated in the caves and perhaps sought such a place when dying. However, he believes it is not likely that a bear would choose such an unusual position in which to lie down and die and that "the skull was placed on the big block by humans."[3] Because of the bear's mythical and supernatural roles in many

---

2 Reverend Elaine Farmer, "Liturgical Tidbits: The Altar."

3 Dr. Jean Clottes, *Chauvet Cave*, 204.

cultures, Dr. Clottes suggests that the bear may have been deified by the Paleolithic people who used the cave.

Undisputed evidence of altars comes from the Neolithic period. Agriculture allowed populations to stabilize and settle in one place, ushering in major changes to human culture. The city-state of Megiddo,[4] founded circa 6000 BCE at a strategic location along an ancient Middle Eastern trading route, contains a large altar of the earliest type mentioned in the Bible: a mound of earth or stone. The religious complex at Megiddo contains a sacrificial altar that is almost thirty-three feet in diameter. Steps lead up to the platform top, which is five feet high. According to archaeologists, this fits the description of a "high place" mentioned in the Bible. "Horned" altars were also found at Megiddo.[5]

At the prehistoric settlement of Lepenski Vir (6500–5500 BCE) along the Danube in Serbia and Montenegro, rectangular stone altars were surrounded by flooring of V-shaped stones. Statues and receptacles for offerings were discovered along with the bones of fish, red deer, dogs, and wild boar. In their artwork, the people of Lepenski Vir portrayed dogs and boars as attendants of the goddess of death, while fish and deer represented the goddess's aspects of birth and regeneration. Some of these altars are plain, while others are incised with circles and zigzags. One altar is shaped like the head of a fish, and two others suggest the shape of a deer.[6]

Temple altars of the Sesklo culture (6000–5800 BCE) in Achilleion, Greece, held ceramic figurines portraying a bird goddess and a snake goddess. Large libation vases were found beside the altars. The temple courtyards contained stone altars as well as circular hearths. In western Romania, three table-like altars of earth and clay dating to around 5000 BCE held sculptures, pan-shaped containers, and vases. In western Ukraine,

---

4 Megiddo is an archaeologist's dream, with multiple layers of habitation that span continuous occupation from 6000 BCE to 500 CE. The name *Armageddon* means *Hill of Megiddo*, according to *Encyclopedia Britannica Micropaedia*, 15th ed., s.v. "Megiddo."

5 Magnus Magnusson, *Archaeology of the Bible*, 184.

6 Marija Gimbutas, *The Civilization of the Goddess*, 284–285.

shrine rooms with rectangular altars also contained bread ovens (4800–4600 BCE), which archaeologists interpreted as providing sacred bread with which to honor the mother/provider goddess.[7]

In the ancient Sumerian city of Eridu (present-day Iraq), a temple of mud brick on a raised platform housed an altar and a freestanding offering table in the rectangular sanctuary. By 2200 BCE, temples were increasing in size and height (seventy-five feet high) and eventually evolved into the *ziggurats*, terraced pyramidal temples constructed of successively smaller tiers. The top terrace of the ziggurat contained "God's little shrine," accessible only to priests.[8] The best-preserved ziggurat, in the city of Ur, was built circa 2100 BCE. Its lower stage measures 210 by 150 feet. The hanging gardens of Babylon were ziggurats outfitted with trees and plants to make them resemble natural hills.

On the island of Malta in the Mediterranean, the temple complex at Hagar Qim (3000–2000 BCE) contains two table-shaped altars and a pillar altar with a carved decoration of a tree growing from a vase. Other temple altars are decorated with spirals, triangles, and a snake—symbols of vital life-force energy. Another altar is flanked by two stone pillars, with a third behind the altar. One altar at the Tarxien temple is decorated with images of a ram, a sheep, and a pig, suggesting animal sacrifice. Archaeologists have found evidence of burned sacrifices. Seashells were also offered up to the Divine. On the nearby island of Gozo, the altars in the Ggantija temple (circa 3000 BCE) consist of great stone slabs, two of which stand upright and support a horizontal third to create a tabletop.

Constructed by human hands, Silbury Hill, about sixteen miles north of Stonehenge in England, fits the bill for "high places" and is the largest prehistoric structure in Europe (circa 2700 BCE). Built of clay and chalk rubble and covered with topsoil and turf, Silbury stands approximately 110 feet high. It has been suggested that the flattened top served as a

---

7 Marija Gimbutas, *The Language of the Goddess*, 133.

8 *Encyclopedia Britannica Micropaedia*, 15th ed., s.v. "Ziggurat."

giant altar where grain and other agricultural goods were offered to the Mother Goddess in thanks for a good harvest.

The so-called altar stone of Stonehenge, buried under a fallen sarsen and lintel, is believed by archaeologists to have been an upright pillar stone rather than a horizontal altar. In contrast, the "recumbent-stone" circles of Scotland and Ireland (2300–1800 BCE) contain at least one stone larger than the others that was intentionally placed horizontally.[9] These potential altars are usually of rock that is geologically different from the standing stones and are always located along the south-southwest quadrant of the circle.

In Norfolk, England, the ancient flint mine (2800–2500 BCE) called Grimes Graves contains a carved altar ledge upon which a carved chalk goddess figurine and a phallus, also of chalk, were found. Picks of deer antler that were used for mining were piled nearby.

The stump of an old oak tree served as an altar at the center of a fifty-five-post circle known as Seahenge (2050 BCE) on the coast of Norfolk. The oak stump had been planted upside down so that its remaining roots created an altar table. Archaeologists found that the wood had been worked with bronze axes.

A common feature of many Neolithic sites throughout England, Scotland, and Ireland, as well as Austria and Switzerland, are rocks with cup-mark indentations. Archaeologists have speculated that these stones were used for offering libations. The cup marks are frequently accompanied by spirals and circles carved into the stone. Temple altar stones on Sardinia (1200–200 BCE) frequently have a large circle carved into their tops and are also believed to have been used for offering libations. In addition, these altars appear to be aligned with the summer solstice's sunrise.

On the island of Menorca off the coast of Spain, stone structures called *navetas*, resembling upturned boats, were constructed between 1800 and 1500 BCE. Some had been used for burial chambers and others

---

9 Alastair Service and Jean Bradbery, *The Standing Stones of Europe*, 197.

for dwellings. Opposite the entrance, all had built-in ledges that are believed to have been used as altars.[10]

The ancient Egyptians had a complex array of gods and goddesses to represent the natural forces. Religion and ritual held a central position in everyday life—and death. Altars were placed in tombs with offerings of meat and drink in order for the deceased's *ka*—the double or spirit body that continued to live in the tomb—to be cared for.[11] People who were too poor to afford an altar for their tomb or the offerings to place upon it had a small model altar made from stone. Clay models of food have been found with these altars. In a real pinch, a picture of an altar with offerings was painted and placed in the tomb.

Large altars in offering halls (the room preceding the sanctuary) were used to make sacrifices. Other small altars stood within the sanctuaries. Large temple complexes had multiple altars in courtyards and halls. In the temples, offerings of food, libations, and flowers were made twice daily by priests. With images of gods and goddesses, altars and temples provided a tangible place and form through which offerings could be channeled to the deities.

Altars' size and style varied widely. Some were simple and made of cubical blocks of basalt or granite, some were carved and decorated, and others were flat slabs (or slabs containing slight depressions) resting on cylindrical pedestals. Some were low tables and others were tall, flat-topped structures that were accessible by a staircase built into one side. Some altars had hidden chambers below them, from which priests would give "oracular pronouncements."[12] Altars found at Luxor and Karnak had raised corners, which would later be referred to as the "horns" of the altar. These horns were believed to symbolize life, fertility, and protection.[13]

---

10 Ibid., 132.

11 The ancient Egyptians believed that a person's double would continue to live and remain in the tomb with the physical body. E. A. Wallis Budge, *Egyptian Magic*, 105–107.

12 Richard H. Wilkinson, *The Complete Temples of Ancient Egypt*, 136.

13 Ibid., 78.

At Abu Ghurub, outside a temple dedicated to the sun god Re, stands a large calcite altar that was created with the shapes of four *hetep* hieroglyphs (symbol for offering) around a central circular platform that symbolizes the sun.[14] In another great solar temple at Amarna, the interior chambers were filled with hundreds of small altars.

Altars are also depicted in Egyptian art. For example, a bas-relief of Pharaoh Akhenaten (1369–1332 BCE) and his chief wife, Nefertiti, are shown standing at a simple altar making offerings of flowers to the god Aten. Home altars were used for personal offerings of food, libations, and flowers, and incense burners in the shape of miniature altars were common.

Like the Egyptians, the ancient Greeks and Romans had a complex hierarchy of gods and goddesses. Household gods were an important part of religious life. Individuals and families would dedicate themselves and their altars to one or two deities. An exception was discovered at Oropus, a Greek seaport, where an altar was divided into five parts, with each part dedicated to a different group of gods and goddesses. Household altars were dedicated to the family's ancestors and frequently held small bronze and clay figurines of deities.

The altars of Greece took many shapes and sizes—round or square, and frequently with sculpted ornamentation. Symbols included the head and horns of oxen. Altars for burnt offerings were located out of doors in courtyards, but when part of a temple, they stood in an enclosed courtyard at the eastern end of the building.

Altars for celestial gods and goddesses were table height or higher, whereas altars dedicated to chthonic deities were low to the ground. The most important gods and goddesses had great temples dedicated to them. These include the Parthenon in Athens to Athena and the complex at Delphi to Apollo. The famous Pergamon altar, perched atop a great acropolis in what is now Bergama, Turkey, was a huge structure dedicated to Zeus (180–160 BCE). The altar proper was surrounded by a colonnade of Ionic

---

14 Ibid., 120.

pillars at the top of a large, wide staircase. Saint John made reference to this altar as "Satan's seat."[15]

In Roman homes, the altar was frequently placed near the hearth—a common practice in earlier Neolithic settlements such as Catal Hüyük in Turkey (6000–5000 BCE).

Second- and third-century Roman temples showed Greek influence; however, altars were located inside temples rather than in outdoor courtyards. Like the Greeks, Roman celestial deities were honored with raised altars, and chthonic deities with low altars, which occasionally occupied an excavated area below floor level.

Around 90 CE, the Roman worship of Mithras (from Zoroastrianism, the pre-Islamic religion of Iran) arose, and many altars and temples were dedicated to him. A decorated altar with a personal inscription to Mithras (circa 130 CE) was discovered in Carrawburgh, one of several temples to Mithras along Hadrian's Wall in Scotland. Many of the altars were carved in the shape of square pillars. These temples had multiple altars, one of which was used for the ritual of serving bread and wine.[16] Altars to the gods Jupiter and Mars were also found along Hadrian's Wall. In addition, permanent altars with burning fires were depicted on coins.

In the Americas, the most well-known ancient altars were the sacrificial altars atop elaborately decorated pyramids. The Aztec believed that the gods were nourished by human hearts and that the continued existence of the world depended on the gods receiving blood sacrifice.[17]

In the great Olmec city of Teotihuacan (circa 300–700 CE), near present-day Mexico City, raised platforms were used for ritual. The city's name means "place of the gods."[18] The Maya built pyramids on hilltops, where it was believed that "gods once came to earth."[19] Up until approx-

---

15 Edward Norman, *House of God*, 24.

16 This practice was a sore point for Christians, who saw it as a blasphemy of their Communion. Dr. David J. Breeze, *Hadrian's Wall*, 31.

17 Jonathan Norton Leonard, *Ancient America*, 103.

18 Ibid., 36.

19 Ibid., 31.

imately 600 CE, the Mochica of Peru built adobe brick temples topped with shrines, where offerings of seashells were found by archaeologists.

Beginning in the Middle East

The early Semites venerated Ashtoreth, who was worshipped as an equal to God. She was a goddess who represented the nurturing earth and was usually symbolized with a tree. Altars to Yahweh were located beside a sacred tree or "tree-like post," depicting the relationship of goddess and god.[20]

According to Leslie Parrott, altars are mentioned 433 times in the Bible.[21] The Old Testament mentions that early altars were in the open and frequently on hilltops or higher ground in places where deity was manifest or invoked for a purpose. Evolving from a mound (natural or artificial), the altar became a platform above the floor where offerings could be lifted to the Divine. Also according to Parrott, the Hebrews sanctified their altar and it "became the place of spiritual renewal through prayer, praise, sacrifice and commitment."[22]

According to the Bible, Noah constructed an altar in gratitude to God after surviving the flood. Abraham and Sarah built a number of altars on their journey, and Moses, receiving instructions from God, built a simple one. The continued use of private altars was permitted as long as they followed the proscribed construction using "unhewn stones." However, after the Israelites flirted with disaster and Yahweh's wrath with their altars to Ba'al and Ashtaroth, the situation changed. The laws of Deuteronomy centralized worship into the temple and of one god. Sacrifice had to be done at the temple to avoid idolatry and to suppress Pagan ways. The use of high places, steps, and extraneous ornamentation was condemned—at least for a while.

---

20 Nathaniel Altman, *Sacred Trees*, 44.
21 Leslie Parrott, *Softly and Tenderly*, 30.
22 Ibid., 35.

The great temple of Solomon in Jerusalem is believed by Christians and Jews to be the site of the altar where Abraham was prepared to sacrifice Isaac. At the time of Solomon's temple, two types of altars came into use: the altar of burnt offerings and the altar of incense. The altar of burnt offerings, also called the altar of holocaust or the brazen altar, contained a perpetual fire that heated the stones upon which the sacrifice was seared. This altar stood outside, at the east entrance of the temple, and was said to have been fifteen feet high and thirty feet long.

The practice of blood sacrifice was believed by the ancient Jewish people to provide a link between humans and God and to allow people to atone for their sins. Offering meat to God was accomplished by cooking or burning it, as it was believed that God took his portion by inhaling the smoke and aroma. A perpetual fire on the altar—the hearth of the temple—was a symbolic way to represent the presence of God, and eventually the altar itself came to represent his presence and was considered holy. Because of this representation, the altar is where important vows were—and still are—taken. Vows performed at an altar were understood to be more completely binding.

The altar of burnt offerings was usually rectangular in shape and had four horns—one at each corner, like some of the Egyptian altars. The horns were a sign of power and were regarded as the most sacred portion of the altar.[23] During the annual rite of purification, they were wiped with blood. The fire on the altar of burnt offerings evolved into other utensils, such as fire-pans, which were, in turn, replaced by large candles when blood sacrifice was no longer carried out.

The other type of altar, the altar of incense or perfumes, was located inside the temple. Originally created from bricks of baked earth, these altars were later made of limestone. They could be rectangular or cylindri-

---

23 Anyone in contact with the altar or in close proximity was considered to be under the protection of God. The Bible (1 Kings 1:50) describes an asylum seeker taking hold of the horns of the altar and declaring his intent. In Revelations, the altar is called a place of eternal safety and protection. Catholic University of America, *The New Catholic Encyclopedia*, 345.

cal in shape. The altar of incense in Solomon's temple was said to have been made of gold. Incense was offered at these altars twice a day—in the morning and in the evening.

The offering of incense symbolized the devotion of the soul, while the burnt offerings symbolized the devotion of the body. When Solomon's temple was destroyed and the altars no longer existed, new ways to atone were developed: The study of the Talmud took the place of the altar of incense and acts of charity replaced sacrifice.[24]

The majority of early converts to Christianity came from Judaism, and so the concept of the altar was carried into the new religion. However, rather than represent the presence of God, the altar came to represent the body of Christ. Because of Christ's sacrifice on the cross, making an animal sacrifice to God on the altar was not needed. According to Edward Norman, the altar became a "place for the symbolic re-enactment of his victory over the world."[25]

The simple wooden table-style altar originated in the days when people gathered in private homes. Until the fourth century CE, worship took place wherever safety and privacy could be found. Later, when church buildings were constructed, it was an almost natural progression to have an altar constructed over the tomb of a saint. As Christianity spread, relics were used in other churches to represent martyrs and saints. Where relics were not available, images placed above and behind the altar served the purpose. By the eighteenth century, Baroque sarcophagal altars were extremely ornate.

Large basilicas arrived on the scene when Emperor Constantine adopted Christianity in 312 CE and made it the state religion of the Roman Empire. In North African basilicas, the altar was located in the nave, or body, of the church. In most others, the altars were placed in the semicircular apse that half-enclosed the altar, usually at the eastern end opposite the entrance. It was fairly standard throughout Europe for the church entrance to be in the west, allowing the priest at the altar to face east, where

---

24 Isidore Singer, *The Jewish Encyclopedia*, 467.

25 Edward Norman, *The House of God*, 27.

Christ is believed to appear in his Second Coming. The Vatican II Council (the Reform of the Roman Liturgy, 1963–1965) switched the priest to the opposite side of the altar to face the congregation. Rows of columns flanking the nave created a "sacred way" that led to the altar.[26]

Beginning in the fourth century CE, it became customary for altars to be covered by a canopy (called a *baldacchino* or *civory*[27]) supported with four pillars and to stand behind a protective barrier. As time went on, these became more elaborate and expensive; some were crafted from gold. However, by the tenth century, their use was dwindling except in Italy and in the Eastern Church.

The cultural, theological, and political differences in the Roman Empire led to a split around 1054 CE, and the Greek-speaking Orthodox Church and Latin Roman Catholicism went their separate ways.[28] Altars in the Western Church were rectangular or table-shaped; these were originally free-standing but were later placed against a wall. Some churches had multiple altars, and by the Middle Ages this was common in order to accommodate the growing number of relics. The principal altar was referred to as the "high" altar, perhaps harkening back to very early times.

In the Eastern Church, the building itself represented divine mysteries, and there was only one altar per church. It was square with a wooden top and freestanding, which allowed the clergy to circulate around it. The altar itself was generally unadorned, while the icons placed upon it were highly decorative. In older churches, the altar was separated from the main area by a screen of icons.

In the Western Church, *reredos* or *retablos*, or ornamental panels, on the back of the altar were introduced in the twelfth century to emphasize the importance of reliquaries that were not exactly first class. Any baldacchinos that were still in existence were reconfigured and elevated above the reliquary behind the altar. From the fourteenth to sixteenth centuries,

---

26 Ibid., 24–26.

27 Ibid., 306.

28 Ibid., 40.

retablos became large structures featuring life-sized statues of Christ and Mary. Styles continued to change, and in the seventeenth and eighteenth centuries, arched porticoes—in many cases made of marble—replaced the retablos.

During the Protestant Reformation in the early 1500s, the altar became a symbol of "unreformed doctrine." By 1552, the English prayer book was expunged of the word *altar*. The designation of "Table" or "God's Board" was used for the place where the sacrament was received. The concept of the altar being a place to contact God was gone, but it remains a symbol of the Last Supper and Christ's sacrifice. In England, communion tables were placed "altar-wise," with their long sides facing north-south and narrow ends east-west, and were usually fenced in with rails. Railed altars have gone in and out of style over the centuries. Many Protestant denominations do not have altars, although they have been making a comeback. As with the architecture of post-modern churches and cathedrals, almost anything goes with the design of altars.

The Islamic faith does not employ altars; however, each mosque does have a *mihrab* or special niche. One wall of the mosque called the *qibla* wall faces toward Mecca. At the mid-point, the mihrab is incorporated into the wall. Although the mosque styles vary widely—even being pagoda-shaped in Beijing—the mihrab is usually semicircular with an arched top. It is the most decorated feature and the focal point of a mosque. While the niche itself is not regarded as sacred, the direction in which it points is.[29]

India and Asia

Altars of the Vedic-Aryan period (1500–600 BCE) in India were built according to the Sulva (or Shulba) Sutras, documents written between 800 and 500 BCE from earlier Vedic texts dating back several thousand years.[30] However, while these sutras (teachings) contain detailed information on how to build various altars, actually constructing these altars required

---

29 Martin Frishman and Hasan-Uddin Khan, *The Mosque*, 33.

30 Subhash C. Kak, "The Astronomy of the Age of Geometric Altars," 387.

intricate calculations and a knowledge of geometry. The type of altar depended on the purpose for which it would be used.

Made of mud bricks, these altars were constructed in a wide range of sizes, and some consisted of complicated shapes. The specific size and shape is believed to have provided visual clues for the intricacies of the rituals for which they were built. Some of the altars were in the shape of a circle, semicircle, or square. (Generally, earth was represented by a circle and heaven by a square.) Others had more complex shapes, such as a falcon, heron, or tortoise. These altars, also known as fire altars, had five layers of bricks; each layer had a proscribed number of bricks, the shape of which was also dictated according to which altar was being constructed.

Agni, the god of fire, was represented by these sacrificial altars. (Even today, fire "is a primary symbol of divine energy" in Hindu worship.[31]) Food and oblations were given with the expectation that Agni would take the offering to the god or goddess for whom it was intended. The altars were oriented to the east—sunrise and the domain of Agni. Archaeologists have found evidence of both horse and human sacrifice in relation to these altars. Like the later Buddhist mandalas, these altars themselves were part of the offerings to deities, but rather than being destroyed at the end of ritual, they were simply abandoned.

Classical Hinduism emerged between 300 BCE and 300 CE with different ways of worshipping deities who had evolved from earlier times, and sacrifice became a symbolic rather than actual act. Hindu temples were—and still are—built using the principles of *vastu shastra*, or sacred architecture, a science with roots that date back to approximately 3000 BCE. Like the Vedic altars, Hindu temples are meticulously planned. At the groundbreaking ceremony, a priest invites "the soul of the temple to enter within the building confines"[32] and places a golden box into the ground. The altar, which represents the Cosmic Being, will be positioned above the golden box when the temple is completed.

---

31 Stephen P. Huyler, *Meeting God*, 60.

32 John McLeish, *Number*, 116.

Temple altars range from simple to elaborately carved stone or wood. In addition to images or statues, deity is also represented with a pillar, a round stone, or geometric shapes. Altars are dedicated to a particular deity or group of deities according to denomination. In addition to images or symbols of deity, standard altar equipment includes a lamp to represent the soul or light within, incense to represent desire, offerings of flowers to represent the goodness that blossoms from within, and offerings of fruit to represent sacrifice and surrender. Public shrines and altars also exist without temples in a myriad of places and styles. Platforms of earth and stone are constructed along rivers and under sacred trees and used as altars for offerings.

A stone altar discovered in China that measures sixty by fifty-eight feet and over five feet high dates back to a Neolithic culture (7000–6500 BCE). Other altars constructed of earth walled in with rocks have been found. As with some of the Vedic altars, altars made of earth represented and honored the earth itself.

During the Shang Dynasty (1500–1000 BCE), raised earthen altars were used in ceremonies performed by the emperor. The emperor had the title *T'ien-tzu* ("Son of Heaven") and was responsible for interceding with the gods on behalf of his subjects.[33] Offerings of wine and grains were placed in bronze tripod cauldrons and heated over the altar fire.[34] Evidence of blood sacrifice during this period was also found. Around the eighth century CE, blood sacrifice was replaced with symbolic sacrifice using clay images.[35]

The Xian Altar of Heaven was built during the Sui Dynasty (581–618 CE) and used into the tenth century during the Tang Dynasty. This altar consists of four circular platforms of rammed earth covered in yellow clay and finished with a layer of white paste.

The Xian altar stands 26 feet high with a diameter of 177 feet at its base and 65 feet at the top. Unlike later altars with four staircases, this

---

33 Jacques Gernet, *A History of Chinese Civilization*, 54.
34 Edward Schafer, *Ancient China*, 12.
35 Ibid., 65.

one has twelve, which are believed to represent the twelve parts of heaven as defined by Chinese astronomers. According to Spencer Harrington, the natural materials used for this altar form a stark contrast to the ornamental altars of the Han Dynasty (202 BCE–220 CE).[36]

A number of other large altars have been found in and around Beijing. The Altar of Heaven (also called the Mound Altar) was constructed in 1420 CE and used throughout the Ming (1368–1644) and Ch'ing (1644–1911) dynasties. This round altar has three tiers, each with four white marble staircases with nine steps. According to the ancient Chinese, nine is the number of heaven. The emperor performed ritual on this altar at the winter solstice.

In the late sixth century BCE in what is now Nepal, Buddhism began to spread throughout northern India and Asia. Buddhist altars range from a simple table or stone altar holding an image of the Buddha to elaborately carved shrines. Alternatively, a set of footprints carved or painted on the altar represents the presence of Buddha. The traditional altar consists of three tiers: the top tier for images or statues of Buddha, the second for symbolic elements such as a dharma wheel, and the third for offerings.

According to Malcolm David Eckel, funerary mounds called *stupas* housed relics of the Buddha as well as other great Buddhist teachers. These "served as focal points for worship and meditation."[37] Like altars, stupas were places to leave offerings. In India, some stupas contain sacred texts and prayer wheels in place of relics.

Domestic and Personal Altars

Home altars of Buddhists are as varied as the worshippers who use them. Some denominations have proscribed methods of setup and others do not. In addition to sculptures and symbols placed on altars, paintings, banners, and mandalas are hung behind or alongside them. The altars are simple tables, or three tables of varying heights placed together to cre-

---

36 Spencer P. M. Harrington, "Vintage Altar of Heaven," 18.

37 Malcolm David Eckel, *Buddhism*, 66.

ate three tiers. A small cabinet may sit upon the table to house statues or images, or the entire altar may be enclosed in a small cabinet or large armoire. Personal altar tables from the later dynastic period in China are popular with antique collectors. These altars are finely carved and usually contain several drawers for storing extra ritual goods or sacred items when not in use.

In Japan, family altars called *Butsudans* are used for private worship as well as to honor the dead. An imperial edict in 655 CE declared that each home should include a "court chapel," or sanctuary. By the seventeenth century, household altars were common. A Butsudan is generally recessed into a wall or contained in its own cabinet or "house" (where it houses deity or spirit). These are used in addition to the Shinto *Kamidana* ("god shelf"), where offerings of rice, salt, and water are placed.[38]

Except for festival days, most Hindu worship is not a "congregational activity"; it most often takes place at a shrine in the home.[39] The size of a shrine altar varies greatly. It can occupy an entire room or a tiny niche or simply consist of a row of religious prints on a wall.[40] It can be a large or small cupboard, the doors of which are kept closed when not in use to protect the sacred energy. Images of the Divine are those gods and goddesses important to the household. Small individual altars are also used for personal worship.

While for most Christians the altar is a feature in church, home altars have been a tradition in Hispanic households for centuries. These altars combine sacred objects with belongings of family members who have passed on. These seem to provide a dual function as an expression of a personal relationship with the Divine as well as a visible link between the living and dead.

This practice of a home altar is believed by scholars to have ancient roots in the Mayan practice of keeping domestic altars to honor deity.

---

38 *Encyclopedia Britannica Micropaedia*, 15th ed., s.v. "Butsudan."
39 Stephen P. Huyler, *Meeting God*, 36.
40 Ibid., 42.

Christian symbols eventually replaced indigenous ones or were incorporated into a mélange of religious and personal objects. Although the practice declined slightly in the mid-twentieth century, it has made a strong
comeback because of Latina feminists who have reclaimed the tradition,
which had been held by the female elders.

Preparing Crystals and Gemstones for Use

With new clothes or food, you usually wash them before wearing or eating to ensure that they are clean and not carrying something unwanted. Before using a gemstone, it should be cleansed to remove unwanted or negative energy that it may have picked up through previous handling. Even if you are strongly attracted to a stone, you should cleanse it in order to allow the greatest amount of energy to flow between it and you. Cleaning it will allow a clear, pure flow of energy. It will help you get the most power from the gemstone, too. Over time, you may feel that a stone has lost its potency, which indicates that it needs to be recleaned. Gemstones should be cleaned separately to keep their power focused on their own energy.

Cleansing with salt is advocated especially for gemstones that are new in your life. Sea salt is traditionally recommended; however, this should be a personal decision. Because it comes from the ocean, sea salt is imbued with the power of the waves and the cleansing intention of water. Salt that comes from the earth, the body of Mother Earth, will give the gemstone a strong power for grounding. Make sure to use pure salt; many types on the market contain aluminum or other chemicals.

Another decision to make when salt cleansing is whether to do it wet or dry. For wet cleansing, add a tablespoon of salt to a cup of water. You may start with warm water to dissolve the salt, but let it cool before bathing the gemstone. Water that is too hot may cause the stone to crack and fracture. Use a glass or ceramic container and avoid plastic or metal, as these tend to leach some of their own properties into the water. Allow the gemstone to soak overnight, and then dry it with a soft cloth. For dry cleansing, you will need a container deep enough to fill with salt or soil in order to bury the gemstone. Place the stone in the salt with its point (or top) down, facing the earth, and leave it there overnight.

Another way to cleanse a gemstone is by moonlight. This takes a little longer, but if you want to activate the power of Luna, it's worth the wait. Find a windowsill in your home that gets at least several hours of moonlight during the full moon. Place the gemstone on that windowsill for three nights, beginning with the night before the full moon. Placing the stone on a porch or safe place outside is even better, as the light is not impeded by window glass. To recharge the gemstone from time to time, use the light on the one night of the full moon.

If a gemstone has been used for clearing negativity, place it in a clear glass container of salt water and position it where it will receive the light of a waning moon for several nights. Luna will take the negativity with her as she goes away. A gemstone cleansed in salt water and placed outside (or on a windowsill) on the night of a new moon will be open to receive. The light of a waxing moon will help boost the power of a stone.

A gentle method of cleansing a gemstone is to bury it in a bowl of dried herbs or flower petals. This can be combined with moonlight cleansing, but on its own it takes approximately a week. For extra grounding, bury the gemstone outside in the earth or inside in a cup of soil, with its point or top downward. A speedier way to cleanse a gemstone is through "smudging." In a fireproof bowl or seashell, burn a little sage, cedar, or mugwort and then pass the gemstone through the smoke. You don't need to generate thick smoke for this; a gentle wafting will do nicely. A few lavender flowers can be added for calming energy.

After cleansing a new gemstone, take time to sit with it. Cradle it in your hands and welcome it into your life. Be open to the energy of the stone and establish a connection to it with your own energy. Once you have done this, pass along your intentions for it. Think of how you want to share its energy in your home and call on its powers.

Bibliography

Adiele, Faith. *Meeting Faith: The Forest Journals of a Black Buddhist Nun*. New York: W. W. Norton and Company, 2004.

Altman, Nathaniel. *Sacred Trees: Spirituality, Wisdom and Well-Being*. New York: Sterling Publishing, 2000.

Ann, Martha, Dorothy Imel, Lee Redfield, and Barbara J. Suter. *The Great Goddess: An Introduction to Her Many Names*. Boulder, CO: Our Many Names, 1993.

Arrien, Angeles. *The Four Fold Way: Walking the Paths of the Warrior, Teacher, Healer and Visionary*. San Francisco: HarperSanFrancisco, 1993.

Artress, Lauren. *Walking a Sacred Path: Rediscovering the Labyrinth as a Spiritual Tool*. New York: Riverhead Books, 1995.

Asimov, Isaac. *Asimov on Numbers*. Garden City, NY: Doubleday & Company, 1977.

Atkinson, R. J. C. *Stonehenge and Neighboring Monuments*. London: English Heritage, 1987.

Attenborough, David. *The First Eden: The Mediterranean World and Man*. Boston: Little, Brown and Company, 1987.

Ballou, Robert O., ed. *The Portable World Bible*. New York: Penguin, 1976.

Baltsan, Hayim. *Webster's New World Hebrew Dictionary* (Transliterated). New York: Prentice Hall, 1992.

Beer, Robert. *The Handbook of Tibetan Buddhist Symbols*. Boston: Shambhala Publications, 2003.

Berg, Michael. *The Way: Using the Wisdom of Kabbalah for Spiritual Transformation and Fulfillment*. New York: John Wiley & Sons, 2001.

Blum, Ralph H. *The Book of Runes: A Handbook for the Use of an Ancient Oracle; The Viking Runes*. Los Angeles: Oracle Books, 1982.

Bowman, Catherine. *Crystal Awareness*. St. Paul, MN: Llewellyn, 1997.

Breeze, David J. *Hadrian's Wall*. London: English Heritage, 1988.

Brown, C. MacKenzie. *The Devi Gita: The Song of the Goddess; A Translation, Annotation, and Commentary*. Albany, NY: State University of New York Press, 1998.

Budge, E. A. Wallis. *Egyptian Magic*. New York: Dover Publications, 1971.

Buehrens, John A., and F. Forrester Church. *Our Chosen Faith: An Introduction to Unitarian Universalism*. Boston: Beacon Press, 1989.

Calais-Germain, Blandine. *Anatomy of Movement*. Seattle: Eastland Press, 1991.

Catholic University of America. *The New Catholic Encyclopedia*. Vol. 1. Washington, DC: The Catholic University of America, 1981.

Chiffolo, Anthony F. *100 Names of Mary: Stories & Prayers*. Cincinnati: St. Anthony Messenger Press, 2002.

Clottes, Jean. *Chauvet Cave: The Art of Earliest Times*. Salt Lake City: University of Utah Press, 2003.

Conway, John H., and Richard K. Guy. *The Book of Numbers*. New York: Copernicus/Springer-Verlag, 1996.

Cox, Kathleen. *Vastu Living*. New York: Marlowe & Company, 2000.

Das, Lama Surya. *Awakening the Buddha Within: Tibetan Wisdom for the Western World*. New York: Broadway Books, 1997.

Das, Ram. *Paths to God: Living the Bhagavad Gita*. New York: Harmony Books, 2004.

David-Neel, Alexandra. *Buddhism: Its Doctrines and Its Methods*. New York: St. Martin's Press, 1978.

Davies, D. Gareth, and Chris Saunders. *Verulamium*. St. Albans, UK: Priory Press, 1986.

DeKorne, Jim. *Psychedelic Shamanism*. Port Townsend, WA: Loompanics Unlimited, 1994.

Desai, Prakash N. *Health and Medicine in the Hindu Tradition*. New York: Crossroad Publishing Company, 1989.

Diggs, Dorothy C. *A Working Manual for Altar Guilds*. Wilton, CT: Morehouse-Barlow Company, 1977.

Eckel, Malcolm David. *Buddhism: Origins, Beliefs, Practices, Holy Texts, Sacred Places*. New York: Oxford University Press, 2002.

Ellis, Peter Berresford. *A Brief History of the Druids*. New York: Carroll & Graff Publishers, 2002.

Everett, Thomas H. *The New York Botanical Gardens Illustrated Encyclopedia of Horticulture*. Vol. 9. New York: Garland Publishing, 1982.

Farmer, Elaine. "Liturgical Tidbits: The Altar." Newsletter of St. Paul's Anglican Church, Manuka, Australia, 2004. http://www.stpaulsmanuka.org.au.

Fontana, David. *The Meditator's Handbook: A Comprehensive Guide to Eastern and Western Meditation Techniques*. Rockport, MA: Element Books, 1994.

Franz, Marie-Louise von. *C. G. Jung: His Myth in Our Time*. Translated by William H. Kennedy. New York: G. P. Putnam's Sons, 1975.

Frishman, Martin, and Hasan-Uddin Khan, eds. *The Mosque: History, Architectural Development and Regional Diversity*. New York: Thames and Hudson, 1994.

Fritz, Sandy. *Mosby's Fundamentals of Therapeutic Massage*. 3rd ed. St. Louis: Mosby/Elsevier, 2004.

Gaventa, Beverly Roberts, and Cynthia L. Rigby, eds. *Blessed One: Protestant Perspectives on Mary*. Louisville, KY: Westminster John Knox Press, 2002.

Gernet, Jacques. *A History of Chinese Civilization*. Cambridge: Cambridge University Press, 1990.

Gibson, Clare. *Goddess Symbols: Universal Signs of the Divine Female*. New York: Barnes and Noble, 1998.

Gill, Debbie. *World Religions*. London: Collins, 1997.

Gimbutas, Marija. *The Civilization of the Goddess*. New York: HarperCollins, 1989.

———. *The Language of the Goddess*. New York: HarperCollins, 1991.

Glazier, Michael, and Monika K. Hellwig, eds. *The Modern Catholic Encyclopedia*. Collegeville, MN: Liturgical Press, 1994.

Govert, Johndennis. *Feng Shui: Art and Harmony of Place*. Phoenix, AZ: Daikakuji Publications, 1993.

Graves, Robert. *The White Goddess: A Historical Grammar of Poetic Myth*. New York: Noonday Press, 1997.

Hanson, K. C., and Douglas E. Oakman. *Palestine in the Time of Jesus*. Minneapolis: Fortress Press, 2002.

Harrington, Spencer P. M. "Vintage Altar of Heaven." *Archaeology* 53, no. 2 (March/April 2000). http://www.archaeology.org/0003/newsbriefs/altar.html.

Honore, Pierre. *In Quest of the White God: Mysterious Heritage of South American Civilization*. New York: G.P. Putnam's Sons, 1964.

Horan, Paula. *Empowerment through Reiki*. Twin Lakes, WI: Lotus Light Publications, 1998.

Hulse, David Allen. *The Western Mysteries*. St. Paul, MN: Llewellyn, 2000.

Hultkrantz, Ake. *The Religions of the American Indians*. Translated by Monica Setterwall. Berkeley, CA: University of California Press, 1979.

Huyler, Stephen P. *Meeting God: Elements of Hindu Devotion*. New Haven, CT: Yale University Press, 1999.

Johnsen, Linda. "Beyond God Talk." *Yoga International*, January/February 2006.

Judith, Anodea. *Wheels of Life: A User's Guide to the Chakra System*. St. Paul, MN: Llewellyn, 1993.

Kak, Subhash C. "The Astronomy of the Age of Geometric Altars." *The Quarterly Journal of the Royal Astronomical Society* 36 (1995): 385-396.

Kavasch, E. Barrie. *The Medicine Wheel Garden: Creating Sacred Space for Healing, Celebration and Tranquility*. New York: Bantam Books, 2002.

Kear, Katherine. *Flower Wisdom: The Definitive Guidebook to the Myth, Magic and Mystery of Flowers*. London: Thorsons, 2000.

King, John. *The Modern Numerology: A Practical Guide to the Meaning and Influence of Numbers*. London: Blandford, 1996.

Kulananda. *Principles of Buddhism*. San Francisco: Thorsons, 1996.

Kynes, Sandra. *Gemstone Feng Shui: Creating Harmony in Home and Office*. St. Paul, MN: Llewellyn, 2002.

Lad, Vasant. *The Complete Book of Ayurvedic Home Remedies*. New York: Harmony Books, 1998.

Leeming, David, and Jake Page. *Goddess: Myths of the Female Divine*. New York: Oxford University Press, 1994.

Leonard, Jonathan Norton. *Ancient America*. New York: Time-Life Books, 1967.

Lin, Jami. *The Feng Shui Anthology: Contemporary Earth Design*. Miami: Earth Design Incorporated, 1997.

Lindow, John. *Handbook of Norse Mythology*. Santa Barbara, CA: ABC-CLIO, 2001.

MacEowen, Frank. *The Mist-Filled Path: Celtic Wisdom for Exiles, Wanderers and Seekers*. Novato, CA: New World Library, 2002.

MacKillop, James. *Dictionary of Celtic Mythology*. Oxford: Oxford University Press, 1998.

Magnusson, Magnus. *Archaeology of the Bible*. New York: Simon and Schuster, 1977.

Mandelbaum, Allen, trans. *The Aeneid of Virgil*. New York: Bantam Books, 1985.

Markale, Jean. *The Celts: Uncoverinig the Mythic and Historic Origins of Western Culture*. Rochester, VT: Inner Traditions, 1993.

Marler, Joan, ed. *From the Realm of the Ancestors*. Manchester, CT: Knowledge, Ideas & Trends, 1997.

Matthews, Caitlin, and John Matthews. *The Encyclopedia of Celtic Wisdom: A Celtic Shaman's Sourcebook*. Rockport, ME: Element Books, 1994.

McLeish, John. *Number: The History of Numbers and How They Shape Our Lives*. New York: Fawcett Columbine, 1991.

McNeill, F. Marion. *The Silver Bough: Scottish Folklore and Folk Belief.* Vol. 1. New York: Hyperion Books, 1988.

Migdow, Jeff, and Robyn Ross. *Prana Yoga Teacher Training Manual.* New York: The Open Center, 2000.

Mowat, Farley. *The Alban Quest: The Search for a Lost Tribe.* London: Weidenfeld & Nicolson, 1999.

Nardo, Don. *Greek Temples.* New York: Franklin Watts, 2002.

Norman, Edward. *The House of God: Church Architecture, Style and History.* New York: Thames and Hudson, 1990.

O'Neil, W. M. *Early Astronomy from Babylonia to Copernicus.* Ashford, UK: Sydney University Press, 1986.

Onions, C. T., ed. *The Oxford Dictionary of English Etymology.* Oxford: Oxford University Press, 1991.

Pagels, Elaine. *The Gnostic Gospels.* New York: Random House, 1979.

Parrott, Leslie. *Softly and Tenderly: The Altar; A Place to Encounter God.* Kansas City: Beacon Hall Press of Kansas City, 1989.

Paturi, Felix R. *Prehistoric Heritage.* New York: Charles Scribner's Sons, 1979.

Pegrum, Juliet. *The Vastu Home.* Berkeley, CA: Ulysses Press, 2002.

Pepper, Elizabeth, and John Wilcock. *The Witches Almanac.* Spring 1998–Spring 1999. Newport, RI: Witches Almanac, Ltd., 1998.

———. *The Witches Almanac Spring 2003 Spring 2004.* Newport, RI: The Witches Almanac, Ltd. 2003.

Phillips, Richard. *Numbers: Facts, Figures and Fiction.* Cambridge: Cambridge University Press, 2000.

Prabhavananda, Swami, and Christopher Isherwood, trans. *Bhagavad Gita: The Song of God.* New York: Signet Classic, 2002.

Pyne, Stephen J. *Vestal Fire*. Seattle: University of Washington Press, 1997.

Rohr, Richard, and Andreas Ebert. *Discovering the Enneagram: An Ancient Tool a New Spiritual Journey*. New York: Crossroad Publishing Company, 1992.

Ruiz, Don Miguel. *The Four Agreements*. San Rafael, CA: Amber-Allen Publishing, 1997.

Satchidananda, Sri Swami, trans. and commentary. *The Yoga Sutras of Patanjali*. Buckingham, VA: Integral Yoga Publications, 1978.

Schafer, Edward. *Ancient China*. New York: Time-Life Books, 1967.

Schimmel, Annemarie. *The Mystery of Numbers*. New York: Oxford University Press, 1993.

Service, Alastair, and Jean Bradbery. *The Standing Stones of Europe*. London: George Weidenfeld & Nicolsen, 1979.

Simpson, D. P., ed. *Cassell's Latin Dictionary*. New York: Macmillan Publishing Company, 1978.

Singer, Isidore. *The Jewish Encyclopedia*. Vol. 1. New York: Funk and Wagnalls Company, 1901.

Smith, B. K. *Reflections on Resemblance, Ritual and Religion*. Oxford: Oxford University Press, 1989.

Sovik, Rolf. "Picture This: Enhancing Meditation with Yantra." *Yoga International*, October/November 2001.

Starhawk. *The Spiral Dance: A Rebirth of the Ancient Religion of the Great Goddess*. San Francisco: HarperSanFrancisco, 1989.

Streep, Peg. *Altars Made Easy*. San Francisco: HarperSanFrancisco, 1997.

———. *Sanctuaries of the Goddess*. New York: Little, Brown and Company, 1994.

Thorsson, Edred. *Futhark: A Handbook of Rune Magic*. York Beach, ME: Samuel Weiser, 1983.

Tigunait, Pandit Rajmani. "The Yoga Sutras." *Yoga International*. January/February 2006.

Trigilio, John Jr., and Kenneth Brighenti. *Catholicism for Dummies*. Hoboken, NJ: Wiley Publishing, 2003.

Walker, Barbara G. *The Women's Encyclopedia of Myths and Secrets*. San Francisco: HarperSanFrancisco, 1983.

Warren-Clarke, Ly. *The Way of the Goddess*. Bridport, UK: Prism Press, 1987.

Webber, F. R. *Church Symbolism*. Detroit: Gale Research Co., 1971.

Wickersham, John M., ed. *Myths and Legends of the World*. Vol. 1. New York: Macmillian Reference USA, 2000.

Wilkinson, Richard H. *The Complete Temples of Ancient Egypt*. New York: Thames and Hudson, 2000.

Yogananda, Paramahansa. *Inner Peace: How to Be Calmly Active and Actively Calm*. Los Angeles: Self-Realization Fellowship, 1999.

Yogani. *Deep Meditation: Pathway to Personal Freedom*. Nashville, TN: AYP Publishing, 2005.

Index

LLEWELLYN ORDERING INFORMATION

Order Online:
Visit our website at www.llewellyn.com, select your books, and order them on our secure server.

Order by Phone:
- Call toll-free within the U.S. at 1-877-NEW-WRLD (1-877-639-9753). Call toll-free within Canada at 1-866-NEW-WRLD (1-866-639-9753)
- We accept VISA, MasterCard, and American Express

Order by Mail:
Send the full price of your order (MN residents add 6.5% sales tax) in U.S. funds, plus postage & handling to:

Llewellyn Worldwide
2143 Wooddale Drive, Dept. 978-0-7387-1105-8
Woodbury, MN 55125-2989

Postage & Handling:

Standard (U.S., Mexico, & Canada). If your order is:
$24.99 and under, add $3.00
$25.00 and over, FREE STANDARD SHIPPING

AK, HI, PR: $15.00 for one book plus $1.00 for each additional book.

International Orders (airmail only):
$16.00 for one book plus $3.00 for each additional book

Orders are processed within 2 business days.
Please allow for normal shipping time. Postage and handling rates subject to change.

Whispers from the Woods

The Lore & Magic of Trees

SANDRA KYNES

A walk in the woods makes it easy to understand the awe and reverence our ancestors had for trees. It speaks to something deep and primal within us—something we don't hear as often as we should.

By exploring a variety of mysteries and traditions of trees, *Whispers from the Woods* helps readers get reacquainted with the natural world and find their place in the earth's rhythm. Covering more than just Celtic Ogham and tree calendars, this book includes meditation, shamanic journeys, feng shui, spellcraft, and ritual. In addition, it has a reference section with detailed information on fifty trees, which includes seasonal information, lore, powers, attributes, and more.

Sandra Kynes (New Jersey) is an artist and explorer of Celtic history, myth, and magic. She is a member of the Order of Bards, Ovates and Druids, as well as the Covenant of Unitarian Universalist Pagan Society (CUUPS). She also leads workshops and teaches about ritual at her local congregation.

978-0-7387-0781-5
288 pp., 7 $^1/_2$ x 9 $^1/_8$ $17.95

A Year of Ritual

Sabbats & Esbats for Solitaries & Covens

SANDRA KYNES

It's easy to lose ourselves in the everyday business of life. One way to bring our bodies, minds, and spirits into alignment is through ritual celebrations. A vital part of Wicca and Paganism, ritual strengthens our connection to nature and helps us to enter the realm of the Divine.

For Witches and Pagans of all levels, *A Year of Ritual* provides ready-made rituals for a full year of Sabbats and Esbats. Groups or solitary participants can use these easy-to-follow rituals straight from the book. Ideas, words, and directions for each ritual are included along with background information, preparation requirements, and themes. This unique sourcebook also explains basic formats and components for creating your own rituals.

978-0-7387-0583-5
240 pp., 7 ¹/₂ x 9 ¹/₈ $14.95

Goddess Alive!

Inviting Celtic & Norse Goddesses into Your Life

MICHELLE SKYE

The seasons, moon phases, and even our personal experiences can be linked to the Divine Feminine. They have a face . . . they have a name . . . they have a goddess!

Meet thirteen vibrant Celtic and Norse goddesses very much alive in today's world. Explore each deity's unique mythology and see how she relates to Sabbats and moon rites. Lyrical meditations will guide you to otherworldly realms where you'll meet Danu, the Irish mother goddess of wisdom, and Freya, the Norse goddess of love and war. As you progress spiritually, you'll begin to see Aine in the greening of the trees and recognize Brigid in a seed's life-giving potential.

Goddess Alive! also includes crafts, invocation rituals, and other magical activities to help you connect with each goddess.

978-0-7387-1080-8
288 pp., 7 1/2 x 9 1/8 $18.95

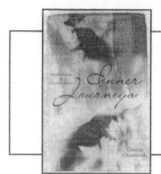

Inner Journeys

Meditations and Visualizations

GLORIA CHADWICK

Winding down after a long day often means turning on the television, opening a beer, or tearing into a pint of Chunky Monkey. A more productive, calorie-free way to chase away tension, anxiety, and the daily blahs is through meditation.

In *Inner Journeys*, Gloria Chadwick introduces the art of meditation and its rejuvenating effect on the mind, body, and spirit. This book features three kinds of meditations—unguided, self-guided, and guided visualization—and discusses how to practice each. These meditations and visualizations are designed to help you quiet distracting mind chatter, focus inward, and explore the limitless realm of your heart and soul. Learn firsthand how this increasingly popular practice can help you reduce stress, uplift your mood, rediscover the magic of childhood, boost intuition and creativity, uncover insights and hidden feelings, achieve spiritual awareness, and illuminate your true self.

Gloria Chadwick is a writer and teacher with more than thirty years of experience. Through her books and workshops, she has helped thousands of people learn to meditate.

978-0-7387-0898-0
168 pp., 6 x 9 $12.95

Spanish edition:
El arte de la meditación
978-0-7387-1046-4 $12.95

To order, call 1-877-NEW-WRLD
Prices subject to change without notice

Crystal Awareness
CATHERINE BOWMAN

This introduction to crystals has become a trusted guidebook for more than 150,000 readers. Crystals are beautiful, powerful gifts from the earth, here to teach and serve us. *Crystal Awareness* covers the basics of crystal work for physical and spiritual healing, increased energy, greater intuition, dream guidance, and protection. It even shows you how to craft your own crystal jewelry.

Learn the nature of crystals and their different forms and powers. What type of crystal should you use for healing? How can you use clusters of crystals? What are the effects of small crystals versus large ones? The answers are here.

You will also discover how crystal energy fields can interact with your personal energy fields and how to use crystals in meditation to open you to deeper personal awareness.

978-0-87542-058-5
224 pp., 4³/₁₆ x 6⁷/₈, illus. $5.99

Homeopathy

An A to Z Home Handbook

ALAN V. SCHMUKLER

Effective, safe, affordable, and free of chemical side effects—the benefits of homeopathy are endless! Already established in the national health care systems of England, France, Germany, and the Netherlands, homeopathic treatments are used by over 500 million people worldwide. Alan Schmukler's *Homeopathy* discusses the history and science of this alternative medicine and provides a comprehensive list of proven remedies—safe for people *and* animals.

Packed with homeopathic treatments for arthritis, colds, food poisoning, insomnia, Lyme disease, morning sickness, wounds, and a host of other ailments and injuries, this handy reference guide also includes information on homeopathic immunization and first aid. Schmukler gives helpful instructions for matching remedies with symptoms, ingesting them correctly, making remedies at home, and stretching your supply.

Alan V. Schmukler (Philadelphia, PA) taught homeopathy at Temple University and has been lecturing on the subject for over a decade. He founded the Homeopathic Study Group of Metropolitan Philadelphia and has contributed to the newsletter *Homeopathy News and Views*.

978-0-7387-0873-7
360 pp., 6 x 9 $16.95

Sticks, Stones, Roots & Bones

Hoodoo, Mojo & Conjuring with Herbs

STEPHANIE ROSE BIRD

Learn the art of everyday rootwork in the twenty-first century. Hoodoo is an eclectic blend of African traditions, Native American herbalism, Judeo-Christian ritual, and magical healing. Tracing Hoodoo's magical roots back to West Africa, Stephanie Rose Bird provides a fascinating history of this nature-based healing tradition and gives practical advice for applying Hoodoo magic to everyday life. Learn how sticks, stones, roots, and bones—the basic ingredients in a Hoodoo mojo bag—can be used to bless the home, find a mate, invoke wealth, offer protection, and improve your health and happiness.

978-0-7387-0275-9
288 pp., 7 ¹/₂ x 9 ¹/₈, illus. $14.95

Meditation as Spiritual Practice
GENEVIEVE L. PAULSON

Meditation has many purposes: healing, past life awareness, mental clarity, and relaxation. This practice can also enhance our spiritual lives by bringing about "peak experiences" or transcendental states. *Meditation as Spiritual Practice* focuses on the practice of meditation for expanding consciousness and awareness. The techniques in this treasured guidebook can also help one in developing clairvoyance, clairaudience, and other psychic abilities.

978-0-7387-0851-5
224 pp., 6 x 9 $12.95

To order, call 1-877-NEW-WRLD
Prices subject to change without notice

Practical Guide to Creative Visualization

Manifest Your Desires

DENNING & PHILLIPS

All things you want must have their start in your mind. The average person uses very little of the full creative power that is potentially his or hers. If you can see it . . . in your mind's eye . . . you will have it! It's true: you can have whatever you want, but there are "laws" to mental creation that must be followed. The power of the mind is not limited to, nor limited by, the material world. Creative visualization enables humans to reach beyond, into the invisible world of astral and spiritual forces.

Some people apply this innate power without actually knowing what they are doing, and achieve great success and happiness; most people, however, use this same power, again unknowingly, incorrectly, and experience bad luck, failure, or, at best, an unfulfilled life.

This book changes that. Through an easy series of step-by-step, progressive exercises, your mind is applied to bring desire into realization! Wealth, power, success, happiness, even psychic powers . . . even what we call magickal power and spiritual attainment . . . all can be yours. You can easily develop this completely natural power, and correctly apply it, for your immediate and practical benefit.

978-0-87542-183-4
240 pp., 5³/₁₆ x 8 $10.95

Spanish edition:
Guía práctica a la visualización creativa
978-1-56718-204-0 $9.95

To order, call 1-877-NEW-WRLD
Prices subject to change without notice

To Write to the Author

If you wish to contact the author or would like more information about this book, please write to the author in care of Llewellyn Worldwide and we will forward your request. Both the author and publisher appreciate hearing from you and learning of your enjoyment of this book and how it has helped you. Llewellyn Worldwide cannot guarantee that every letter written to the author can be answered, but all will be forwarded. Please write to:

Sandra Kynes
c/o Llewellyn Worldwide
2143 Wooddale Drive, Dept. 978-0-7387-1105-8
Woodbury, MN 55125-2989, U.S.A.
Please enclose a self-addressed stamped envelope for reply,
or $1.00 to cover costs. If outside U.S.A., enclose
international postal reply coupon.

Many of Llewellyn's authors have websites with additional information and resources. For more information, please visit our website at:
www.llewellyn.com

CPSIA information can be obtained at www.ICGtesting.com
Printed in the USA
LVOW11s0235170715

446386LV00007B/20/P